Securities and Capital Markets Regulation in South Africa

International Banking and Securities Law

Volumes published in this Brill Research Perspectives title are listed at *brill.com/rpbs*

Securities and Capital Markets Regulation in South Africa

A Contemporary View

By

C. King Chanetsa

BRILL

LEIDEN | BOSTON

This paperback book edition is simultaneously published as issue 3.1 (2018) of *International Banking and Securities Law*, DOI:10.1163/24056936-12340007.

Library of Congress Control Number: 2019945492

Typeface for the Latin, Greek, and Cyrillic scripts: "Brill". See and download: brill.com/brill-typeface.

ISBN 978-90-04-39588-6 (paperback)
ISBN 978-90-04-41305-4 (e-book)

This book is printed on acid-free paper and produced in a sustainable manner.

Contents

Securities and Capital Markets Regulation in South Africa

A Contemporary View

C. King Chanetsa
Chanetsa Inc.
wordsmith@global.co.za

Abstract

An effective securities and capital markets industry has existed in South Africa for over 120 years. The regulatory authorities have been alive to globally competitive pressures for inward investment and have endeavoured to implement a conducive environment therefore in compliance with international standards. As recently as 2015, South Africa was considered the best regulator of securities in the world. The effects of the global financial crisis (GFC) were keenly observed. The fall out from the GFC contained lessons for all markets, but not to the same extent. Commentators may therefore regard aspects of the South African reform agenda as replicative of initiatives in other jurisdictions and, consequently, uncritical in parts. In light of the fall to forty sixth place in the world in securities regulation ranking and some uncertainty in respect of the extent and shape of the reform process, this opus reviews activities in South Africa along the busy securities and capital markets value chain, and considers the continuing and emerging regulatory and supervisory framework.

Keywords

securities and capital markets – regulation – reform – risk based supervision – enforcement – best practice – standards

Introduction

Over the last 10 years, securities and capital markets the world over have experienced upheavals and disruptions to a greater or lesser extent, depending

 | DOI:10.1163/9789004413054_002

on whether the markets were located in developed, developing or emerging markets. This was directly attributable to far-reaching economic distress, the plunging of financial indices and general loss of investor confidence emanating from the GFC. Markets have largely recovered but remain vulnerable to fluctuating fundamentals. The purpose of this opus is to present an overview of securities and capital markets regulation and supervision in South Africa and, in the process, highlight the context and motivation for the significant reforms currently underway. The reader should be mindful of the reality that whilst company law in South Africa is relatively settled and predictable, securities law, often regarded as a specialised branch of company law, is a developing field dominated by emerging regulation fuelled by policy considerations rather than case law.

Part A – Regulation

1 *Background*

During the year 2008–2009, regulation of securities in South Africa was ranked fifth best in the world by the World Economic Forum (WFE). The next year (2010–2011), it was ranked first, a noteworthy position it held for 5 successive years until 2014–2015. It dropped one place to second in 2015–2016, another place to third in 2016–2017, and a suffered a steep decline to forty sixth place in 2017–2018.[1]

Securities regulation is a significant cog in the wheel that drives or hinders the greater economy. South Africa has been experiencing significant and well documented uncertainty in its business and investment environment.[2] Amongst other concerns, the jury is still out on the effect, justification or otherwise of the regulatory revamp currently underway in the securities sector. Be that as it may, in the author's view, a plausible new vision can really only be driven by an appropriate, fresh and unshackled outlook which may or may not be achieved in what is looking less and less like a transition (more

1 Klaus Schwab World Economic Forum Global Competitiveness Report. For the latest report see: http://www3.weforum.org/docs/GCR2017-2018/05FullReport/TheGlobalCompetitivenessReport2017%E2%80%932018.pdf. (last visited 13 June 2019). Earlier reports are available on the same site. The WEF asks a very generic question under this category: In your country, to what extent do regulators ensure the stability of the financial market?

2 National Treasury: Reviewing the Regulation of Financial Markets in South Africa, Policy document explaining the Financial Markets Bill, 2011. http://www.treasury.gov.za/public%20comments/FMB/FMB%20policy%20document.pdf. (last visited 13 June 2019). See also Trading Economics: South Africa Rating. https://tradingeconomics.com/south-africa/rating (last visited 13 June 2019).

of a re-branding) from the Financial Services Board (FSB SA) to the Financial Sector Conduct Authority (FSCA).[3]

SA's capital markets developed over time to serve an economy with a diverse base. Ranked by the World Bank as an "upper middle-income country", South Africa is the largest economy in Africa.[4] The economy is mixed, with key sectors roughly contributing to GDP as follows:[5]

a. Agriculture: 2.2 per cent
b. Mining: 10 per cent
c. Manufacturing: 13.3 per cent
d. Electricity and water: 2.6 per cent
e. Construction: 3.9 per cent
f. Wholesale, retail and motor trade, catering and accommodation: 14.6 per cent
g. Transport, storage and communication: 9 per cent
h. Finance, real estate and business services: 20.7 per cent
i. Government services: 17.6 per cent
j. Personal services: 5.9 per cent

Mining in particular can be considered as providing the original platform for the establishment and development of the capital markets in South Africa. The Johannesburg Stock Exchange (JSE) was founded in 1887, one year after the discovery of gold in the Witwatersrand area. This was in response to the need for capital to fund growing investments in the sector. Whilst mining is directly linked to birth of the JSE, it is also a significant factor behind the growth and development of the financial sector in the country. Capital of the magnitude required for large scale projects especially for deep-level gold mining, could really only be sourced effectively on an accommodative exchange platform.[6] A second stock exchange known as the Union Exchange was established in Johannesburg in 1933 and continued to trade until 1958 when it was

3 See discussion infra.

4 Of late, there has been a bit of a seesaw, the subject of friendly banter, between South Africa and Nigeria for top position. See: Nigeria VS South Africa: Which is The Biggest Economy in Africa? https://www.waystocap.com/blog/nigeria-vs-south-africa-which-is-africas-biggest-economy/.

5 See Brand South Africa: SA Economy Overview. https://www.brandsouthafrica.com/investments-immigration/business/economy/south-africa-economy-overview. (last visited 13 June 2019): Percentages are based on third quarter 2015 GDP data from Statistics South Africa.

6 Shakill Hassan: South African Capital Markets: An Overview. https://econrsa.org/publications/working-papers/south-african-capital-markets-overview. (last visited 13 June 2019). Accommodative in the sense of risk based equity financing, rather than more stringent bank funding.

closed by the Treasury.[7] For the last 150 years, public capital markets activity in South Africa has been dominated by the JSE. As at 30 September 2018, 325 companies were listed on the main board of the JSE, and 46 companies were listed on the junior board known as "Alt X". The total market capitalisation of all listed companies on the JSE was R14.3 trillion.[8]

The capital markets winds of change have come to South Africa. This has resulted in the monopoly which the JSE has enjoyed for 60 years being challenged. Between the end of 2016 and 2017, 4 additional stock exchanges were licensed.[9] The landscape for financial market infrastructures including stock exchanges is not one which readily accommodates an unlimited number of players competing for a relatively small pool of investors and issuers. Therefore, the survival or viability of all the new entrants is still to be demonstrated.

Worldwide, except possibly for the USA, corporate finance is still dominated by bank funding. Such funding can be restrictive in view of its usual requirement for collateral and strict and often inflexible covenants in loan agreements. Added to this, it is significant to note the effect of the Basel 3 reforms, which were introduced to improve the banking sector's ability to absorb shocks arising from financial and economic stress.[10] These reforms are, however, expected to result in reduced credit availability or increased cost of credit overall.[11] The Alt X was set up in 2003 as a junior board on the JSE. In common with junior boards in other jurisdictions, Alt X was set up with the aim, amongst other objectives, of facilitating access to the capital markets for small and medium-sized enterprises. It recorded 10 listings in 2004, 7 in 2005, 23 in 2006, 38 in 2007

---

7 South African History Online: The Johannesburg Stock Exchange is Established. https://www.sahistory.org.za/dated-event/johannesburg-stock-exchange-established (last visited 13 June 2019).

8 JSE Market Highlights: https://www.jse.co.za/content/JSEEquityMarketWeeklyStatisticsItems/JSE%20Markets'%20Weekly%20Statistics%2020181026.xlsx. (last visited 13 June 2019). Most of the currency figures in this work are expressed in South African Rand or ZAR. For comparative purposes, the reader should be guided by the following exchange rates: R14.6506: USD; R18.6759: British Pound; and R16.6351: Euro. Current Exchange rates can be obtained from South African Reserve Bank: Current Market Rates. https://www.resbank.co.za/Research/Rates/Pages/CurrentMarketRates.aspx (last visited 13 June 2019).

9 The new exchanges are ZAR X, A2X, Equity Express and 4AX. While the other 3 new entrants are targeting primary and secondary listings along the model of traditional stock exchanges, A2X, which has operational similarities to Chi X and Bats Chi-X has a focus on secondary markets.

10 Bank for International Settlements: Basel 3: A Global Regulatory Framework for More Resilient Banks and Banking Systems. https://www.bis.org/publ/bcbs189.htm. (last visited 13 June 2019).

11 KPMG: Basel 3: Issues and Implications. https://www.iia.nl/SiteFiles/basell-III-issues-implications.pdf. (last visited 13 June 2019).

OVER-ARCHING ACTS	
Financial Sector Regulatory Act (*FSRA*) *Financial Services Board* (*FSB*) *Act* *Financial Intelligence Centre Act* (*FICA*)	
SECTORAL ACTS	
CAPITAL MARKETS (MARKET INTEGRITY)	**INTERMEDIARIES AND FINANCIAL SERVICES PROVIDERS**
–*Financial Markets Act* (*FMA*) –*Companies Act & King 4* –*Collective Investment Schemes Control Act* (*CISCA*) –*Credit Ratings Services Act* (*CRSA*)	–*Financial Advisory & intermediary Services Act* (*FAIS*)
SUBORDINATE LEGISLATION (REGULATIONS AND BOARD NOTICES)	

FIGURE 1

and a high of 74 in 2009.[12] Currently, 64 companies are listed on Alt X. One of the policy drivers for the facilitation of the entry of new operators into the stock exchange space was the desire to increase competition and, in this way, facilitate greater access to capital markets for a wider range of entities.

The lead regulator in securities and capital markets in South Africa is the recently launched FSCA, which replaced the FSB on 1 April 2018. FSCA, together with the South African Reserve Bank (SARB) and the National Credit Regulator, falls under the Ministry of Finance. The National Treasury (NT) is also housed within the Ministry of Finance (MoF) and is responsible for formulating policy for the financial sector.

The primary legislation in the area of capital markets and securities is the Financial Markets Act 19 of 2012 (FMA). Other important legislation in this area includes the Financial Sector Regulation Act 9 of 2017 (FSRA), the Collective Investment Schemes Control Act 45 of 2002 (CISCA) and the Credit Rating Services Act 24 of 2012 (CRSA).[13] The graphic above demonstrates how the over-arching legislation fits in which the sectoral legislation and the subordinate legislation, all of which will be discussed.

12 Alt X Listings Boom Sustainable. https://www.bing.com/search?FORM=BQSBRL&PC=BQ02&q=Basel+3%3A+A+Global+Regulatory+Framework+for+More+Resilient+Banks+and+Banking+Systems.

13 Infra. These Acts will be discussed further in this document.

2 *Periodic Review*

Up until the promulgation of the FMA in 2012, securities and capital market activity was governed by the Securities Services Act of 2004 (SSA). Changes and developments in the industry, especially those driven by technological developments had an influence on the policymakers in South Africa. This included the impact of the changes on the interests of investors, as well as the operations of service providers to the industry. In August 2011, the NT stated:

> Given the economic significance of a well-functioning financial market infrastructure and mindful of economic and regulatory developments both domestically and abroad, the NT considers it timely to comprehensively review the SSA.[14]

The stated purpose of this periodic review was to:

> ensure that the SSA remains sufficiently robust to meet its objectives and the objectives of securities regulation in general.[15]

Quite apart from the need for periodic review, the very public lessons from the GFC which is regarded as having erupted in July 2007,[16] were observed by NT which noted that the GFC had shown what can go wrong when regulatory failure allows exploitation of investors by the financial system.[17] As a consequence, South Africa was committed:

> to a global regulatory reform agenda, which includes a stronger regulatory framework, more effective supervision, improved crisis resolution, and enhanced accountability through international assessments and peer reviews.[18]

---

14 Reviewing the Regulation of Financial Markets in South Africa, Policy Document Explaining the Financial Markets Bill, 2011 supra, page 6.

15 Ibid. page 6.

16 Global Financial Crisis – What Caused it and How the World Responded. Justine Davies June 23, 2017. https://www.canstar.com.au/home-loans/global-financial-crisis.

17 Reviewing the Regulation of Financial Markets in South Africa, Policy document Explaining the Financial Markets Bill, 2011 supra, page 4.

18 Ibid. page 5.

Consequently, the SSA was reviewed against:

(a) the International Organisation of Securities Commissions' (IOSCO) Objectives and Principles of Securities Regulation[19] (IOSCO Principles);

(b) the recommendations of the Financial Sector Stability Assessment which were produced by the International Monetary Fund in August 2008;[20]

(c) the 2008 UNIDROIT Convention on Substantive Rules for Intermediated Securities;[21]

(d) recommendations put forward by the G20 in the wake of the crisis; and

(e) developments in other jurisdictions.[22]

As stated, the FMA is the dominant piece of legislation in securities and capital markets regulation.

In August 2011, the NT released another policy document entitled: "A Safer Financial Sector to Serve South Africa Better."[23] This document, colloquially

---

19 IOSCO's Objectives and Principles for Securities Regulation: https://www.iosco.org/library/pubdocs/pdf/IOSCOPD323.pdf (last visited 13 June 2019).

20 Included in the main recommendations of this assessment, were the following: "Money, foreign exchange, and capital markets: a) enhance surveillance of the OTC forex exchange derivative markets by systematic processing and analysis of information on offshore activity; b) facilitate further development of the stock and bond markets, including by continued measured liberalization of exchange controls calibrated to take account of the macroeconomic situation. Financial sector supervision and regulation: strengthen coordination and information exchange among regulators and policymakers; minimize gaps and overlaps and clearly delineate responsibilities. The FSB SA should develop standards for corporate governance, risk management, and internal controls and harmonize its risk-based models for the different sectors." See IMF South Africa: Financial System Stability Assessment, Including Report on the Observance of Standards and Codes on the following topic: Securities Regulation. https://www.imf.org/external/pubs/ft/scr/2008/cr08349.pdf page 10 (last visited 13 June 2019).

21 Unidroit Convention on Substantive Rules For Intermediated Securities (Geneva, 2009) Last Updated: 27 September 2013. https://www.unidroit.org/instruments/international-sales/103-instruments/capital-markets/capital-markets-geneva-convention/178-unidroit-convention-on-substantive-rules-for-intermediated-securities-geneva-2009.

22 Reviewing the Regulation of Financial Markets in South Africa, Policy Document Explaining the Financial Markets Bill, 2011. supra, page 20. South Africa has been a member of IOSCO since 1998 and has been represented on its board since 2010 initially by the author. As a member of G20, South Africa subjected itself to a Financial Sector Assessment Programme (FSAP) conducted by the World Bank and International Monetary Fund. The Unidroit Convention, supra, takes cognizance "of the growth and development of global capital markets … recognising the benefits of holding securities, or interests in securities, through intermediaries in increasing the liquidity of modern securities markets." As a member of IOSCO, South Africa observes developments in member jurisdictions.

23 National Treasury: http://www.treasury.gov.za/documents/national%20budget/2011/a%20safer%20financial%20sector%20to%20serve%20south%20africa%20better.pdf (last visited 13 June 2019).

known as the "Redbook" followed closely on the earlier policy paper and proposed a roadmap to deal with challenges faced by the financial sector. The Redbook had broader objectives including the maintenance of financial sector stability, protection of consumers as well as ensuring that efficient, effective and inexpensive financial services are made more accessible.[24]

3 *Crisis Review – GFC*

Regulators and finance professionals in South Africa have tracked the causes and effects of the GFC. This was in view of the impact of the GFC on local and international markets and economic fundamentals.[25] These causes and effects included:

(a) the application of "light touch regulation";[26]
(b) aggressive growth and funding strategies in the UK housing market;[27]
(c) excessive risk-taking in the US housing market in a favourable macroeconomic environment;[28]
(d) collateralised debt obligations structured on the back of "sub-prime" mortgages and traded in the markets and the role of credit default swaps which added opacity and increased vulnerability to the financial system;[29]

---

24 Redbook, page 2.

25 A lot has been written elsewhere about events leading up to the crisis. The intention therefore is not to deal with these events in detail in this work.

26 This was a criticism levelled against the Financial Services Authority in the United Kingdom with respect to its oversight of the Royal Bank of Scotland. See Brooke Masters: Regulator's Light Touch Led to Failure. https://www.ft.com/content/2bfi4c52-24ce-11e1-bfb3-00144feabdco. (last visited 13 June 2019). The former Federal Reserve chairman, Alan Greenspan, also conceded that the global financial crisis has exposed a "mistake" in the free market ideology which guided his 18-year stewardship of US monetary policy. See Andrew Clark and Jill Treanor: Greenspan – I was wrong about the economy. Sort of. https://www.theguardian.com/business/2008/oct/24/economics-creditcrunch-federal-reserve-greenspan (last visited 13 June 2019).

27 In a flawed business model, Northern Rock had funded its long-term mortgage loan book primarily from the wholesale market. See The Economist: Northern Rock: Lessons of the Fall. https://www.economist.com/briefing/2007/10/18/lessons-of-the-fall (last visited 13 June 2019).

28 The downturn in the US housing market was a catalyst for a financial crisis that spread from the United States to the rest of the world through linkages in the global financial system. An undeniably favourable feature of the macro-economic environment was the low interest rates. See Reserve Bank of Australia: Global Financial Crisis. https://www.rba.gov.au/education/resources/explainers/the-global-financial-crisis.html. (last visited 13 June 2019).

29 At the time the US government had created policies to facilitate housing for Americans. These policies, through the action of government-sponsored entities (such as Federal Home Loan Mortgage Corporation or Freddie Mac and Federal National Mortgage association or Fannie Mae), were signaling that these entities would purchase mortgages with

(e) the role of hedge funds;[30]
(f) the impact of over-the-counter derivatives.[31]

4 *Crisis Review – Effect on the South African Economy*

At the time of the GFC, South Africa's economy, although relatively small and accounting for less than 1 per cent of the global gross domestic product, was ranked in the top 20 economies by size. In view of its dependence on foreign trade and its need to be able to attract foreign investment, South Africa's economy was not immune to the impact of the economic slowdown caused by the GFC. Slower economic growth in key export markets as well as lower commodity prices and a slowdown in capital flows to developing countries as a whole, impacted the South African economy particularly in the automotive, mining and retail sectors.[32] The GFC therefore, had a severe impact on South Africa. According to the Redbook, South Africa suffered close to 1 million job losses.[33] On the capital markets front, the JSE All-Share index lost 31 per cent between

subprime characteristics. See: Martin Buffet: How do CDOs and CDSs influence the crisis of 2008. Lingnan Journal of Banking, Finance and Economics. http://commons.ln.edu.hk/cgi/viewcontent.cgi?article=1032&context=ljbfe (last visited 13 June 2019).

30 Hedge funds were subjected to a significant amount of criticism at this time. There was an attempt to link their activities to the onset of the GFC. However, whilst the activities of hedge funds were demonstrably linked to earlier crises, it was doubtful whether their activities had caused this particular crisis. See: Stephen Brown: The Role of Hedge Funds in Financial Crises. http://w4.stern.nyu.edu/blogs/sternonfinance/2008/11/the-role-of-hedge-funds-in-fin.html. (last visited 13 June 2019).

31 The dangers of counterparty risk associated with a largely bilaterally cleared market were revealed. "A major problem with bilateral clearing is that it has resulted in a proliferation of redundant overlapping contracts, exacerbating counterparty risk and adding to the complexity and opacity of the interconnections in the financial system. Redundant contracts proliferate because counterparties usually write another offsetting contract, rather than closing them out. All of this has left regulators and other relevant authorities largely in the dark about potential knock-on effects of a major counterparty failure." See: IMF: Making Over-the Counter Derivatives Safer. The Role of Central Counter-Parties. https://www.imf.org/~/media/Websites/IMF/imported-flagship-issues/external/pubs/ft/GFSR/2010/01/pdf/_chap3pdf.ashx. (last visited 13 June 2019). The "sage of Omaha" Warren Buffett famously referred to over-the-counter derivatives as "financial weapons of mass destruction". See: Johnny Hopkins: Derivatives Are Financial Weapons Of Mass Destruction. https://acquirersmultiple.com/2017/02/warren-buffett-derivatives-are-financial-weapons-of-mass-destruction/ (last visited 13 June 2019).

32 Essays, UK: Impact of the Global Economic Crisis on the Automotive Industry. https://www.ukessays.com/essays/economics/impact-of-global-economic-crisis-on-automotive-industry-economics-essay.php. (last visited 13 June 2019).

33 Ibid., page 4.

World Bank: The Impact of the Global Financial Crisis on Financial Markets in Sub-Saharan Africa http://siteresources.worldbank.org/INTAFRSUMAFTPS/Resources/CrisisNote3.pdf, page 3 (last visited 13 June 2013).

July 2008 and April 2009. This was attributed to the JSE's integration with the international financial system rather than inherent weaknesses in the financial system. Also, the South African Rand (ZAR) experienced a sharp depreciation of 23 percent against major currencies in September/October, 2008.[34]

Despite these adverse effects of the GFC, the broader South African financial system was, to a large extent, protected against the direct effects of the GFC. This could be attributed to the fact that:

(a) the regulatory and credit environment was very conservative;
(b) the risk appetite and attendant incentives were less aggressive in South Africa than in the US;
(c) the National Credit Act No. 34 of 2005 protected borrowers;
(d) the South African banking system was well capitalised. For instance, South African banks could gear their capital about 8 times in contrast to US banks which could gear their capital as much as 30 times;
(e) South Africa had implemented Basel 2 successfully, while the US had largely resisted it;
(f) unlike other jurisdictions, funding from foreign sources comprised only about 5 per cent of total funding in the South African banking sector; and
(g) South African banks were prevented by regulation from participating in toxic assets which were at the heart of the US sub-prime crisis.[35]

5 *Crisis Review – Effect on the Economies of Emerging Countries*

The GFC initially affected advanced economies, emerging markets, and low-income countries in very different ways. Advanced economies were affected mainly by the resultant systemic banking crisis. Those emerging markets with well-developed financial systems were initially mostly affected by cross-border financial linkages through reduction in capital flows, volatility in stock market investments, and exchange rates. In the financially less-developed countries the trade effects dominated, with lags.[36]

In addition to the macro economic impacts of the GFC on the US, UK, Eurozone and other advanced economies, the impact on stock markets in particular was far-reaching and systemic. In South Africa, the macroeconomic consequences of the GFC as well as the impact on the market capitalisation of the JSE have been discussed. Other than the impact on the market

34 Ibid., page 3.

35 Dr Hendrik Nel, South African Reserve Bank, Commentary: Financial innovation and a new economics of banking: Lessons from the financial crisis. https://www.resbank.co.za/Lists/News%20and%20Publications/Attachments/51/Hendrik+Nel.pdf.

36 IMF Impact of the Global Financial Crisis on Sub-Saharan Africa. https://www.imf.org/external/pubs/ft/books/2009/afrglobfin/ssaglobalfin.pdf (last visited 13 June 2019).

capitalisation on the JSE, it is difficult to argue that the effects of the global financial crisis on the stock markets were systemic.

South Africa did however experience a number of significant corporate failures which occurred more as a result of reckless and illegal activities, rather than systemic contagion. The following is a sample of the cases: *Dealstream Securities Limited* (concerning single stock futures);[37] *the State vs Joseph Arthur Walter Brown* (fraud and plunder of pension funds);[38] *the Executive Officer: Financial Services Board vs Dynamic Wealth Limited and Others* (illegal collective investment schemes);[39] and *First Strut trading as First Tech* (the largest

37 This company was a non-clearing member of the JSE, authorised to carry out securities services in terms of the SSA and the JSE's rules. It was also an authorised user in terms of the JSE's rules. As a non-clearing member trading futures instruments (single stock futures), it was required to place margin at the JSE through a clearing member (Rand Merchant Bank) which later placed Dealstream in default when it was unable to meet its margin obligations. As the clearing member, Rand Merchant Bank had an obligation to guarantee Dealstreams margin obligations. See Narc Ashton: Dealstream as the FSB Saw IT. https://www.fin24.com/companies/dealstream-as-the-fsb-saw-it-20081008 (last visited 13 June 2019).

38 This case, also known as the "Widows and Orphans" Case, had a number of commonplace fraud facets. One involved the procurement by Brown, under false pretences, of large amounts of capital from clients for the purposes of investment. Brown fraudulently misrepresented that he would safeguard the amounts procured and obtain favourable returns. What happened in fact was that Brown recklessly invested the money for his own benefit. Another facet of this case is that Brown through his company Fidentia Asset Management, entered into a transaction for the purchase of a company, Mercantile Asset Trust Company (MATCO), which administered pension funds, including the investment portfolios underlying those funds. Brown did not have the R93 million purchase price. Despite his undertaking not to exercise control of MATCO until the purchase price had been paid, he took control of MATCO's assets and used R60 million of the funds MATCO was administering to pay the balance of the purchase price. Brown was sentenced to an effective 15 years imprisonment. See The Supreme Court of Appeal of South Africa, case number 681/2013.

39 This was a case in which the Registrar of Collective Investment Schemes had sought an order before the High Court to place Dynamic Wealth Limited under curatorship for operating illegal collective investment schemes without approval and without compliance with important requirements of the CISCA. Non-compliance included failure to produce audited accounts for the investment portfolios. In bringing this action, the Registrar relied, inter alia, upon an inspection report which he had commissioned. Another allegation was that Dynamic Wealth had placed the assets of certain schemes into a company controlled by one member of the Dynamic Wealth Group and issued non-cumulative, non-redeemable preference shares to investors thereby replacing the liquid investments that the investors believed they had. This was done without informing investors and was characterised by the Supreme Court as "blatantly dishonest". Curiously, reliance on the inspection report had not been accepted as competent by the Acting Judge presiding over the case in the High Court, which had also declined to place Dynamic Wealth under curatorship. Significantly, the Supreme Court reversed the High Court holding that the

corporate bond default at the time).[40] Following First Strut's default, the Association for Savings and Investment South Africa (ASISA), which represented asset managers, took the opportunity to expand its two-year enquiry into listing on the bond market. Among other areas, ASISA looked into:

(a) the processes that are followed before and after a listing;
(b) standardising the terminology used in the corporate bond market; and
(c) the covenants, or conditions, that apply when a bond is issued including for example, that a company may not borrow more than a certain amount of its equity.[41]

---

contents of an inspection report were admissible as evidence and that the placement of Dynamic Wealth under curatorship would have been appropriate at the time that the application for this remedy was made. As 2 years had elapsed between the hearings before the High Court and the Supreme Court, the Supreme Court pointed out that it was futile to proceed with the curatorship in the manner applied for. That would have been a classic demonstration of the maxim "brutum fulmen". One of the reasons the urgent application for curatorship had been brought before the High Court in the first instance, was the intention to freeze the substantial assets still held by Dynamic Wealth and to preserve them for the benefit of investors. In the interim between the High Court and Supreme Court judgments, Dynamic Wealth had been unrestricted in its dealings with the assets, thus rendering curatorship futile. See: 2012 (1) SA 453 (SCA).

40 First Strut was the biggest corporate default in South Africa's history. At the time of its liquidation, First Strut's debt was calculated at over R3.5 billion with over 10,000 creditors. First Strut, which had 18 operating companies, employed a modus operandi which was immersed in fraudulent intent and unethical practices, not to mention the mysterious death of its chairman one Jeff Wiggill. Amongst other instances of fraudulent behaviour, it had put up the same asset (plants, print inventory) as security for many of its loans. In other words, these assets were used repeatedly for additional loan funding. In a separate transaction, First Strut had taken over an insolvent construction company known as Cosira, which was involved in the local power utility Eskom's troubled Medupi Project. Cosira was subsequently liquidated. As was subsequently revealed, various asset managers had placed the funds of certain pension funds and collective investment schemes into bonds issued by First Strut and listed on the JSE. These investors were therefore facing losses of approximately R1 billion. Notably, First Strut had no financial records. See Bruce Cameron: First Strut's Web of Deceit Unravels. https://www.iol.co.za/personal-finance/my-money/banking/first-strut-investors-stand-to-lose-r800m-1567468 (last visited 13 June 2019).

41 Bruce Cameron: "First Strut investors stand to lose R 800 million". https://www.iol.co.za/personal-finance/my-money/banking/first-strut-investors-stand-to-lose-r800m-1567468 (last visited 13 June 2019). Asset managers involved in this investment included Investec (R 435 million), Sanlam Capital Markets (R 263 million), Fairtree Capital (R 131 million), Prudential Portfolio Managers (R 51 million), Rand Merchant Bank (R 50 million) and Stanlib Asset Management (R 22 million). See Chantelle Benjamin: "First Struts web of deceit unravels" https://mg.co.za/article/2013-08-02-00-first-struts-web-of-deceit-unravels (last visited 13 June 2019).

The JSE has recently published proposals to amend its rules for debt listings.[42] The additional point is made that there is a dearth of disclosure requirements for JSE listed bond market issuers. The intention of the amendments is to impose "tougher discipline" particularly on state owned entities.[43]

6 *Policy Developments – Background*

South Africa is a former colony of the United Kingdom. It is common cause that it was granted self-determination in a process which excluded the majority of the citizens of the country.[44] The influence of the United Kingdom has remained strong. As demonstrated below, events in the United Kingdom are closely followed, and financial regulatory developments are keenly observed and often adopted:

(a) The South African legal system is largely based on Roman-Dutch law with layers of English common law. The adoption of this hybrid has historical origins. Dutch settlers arrived in the area known as the Western Cape of South Africa in the mid-seventeenth century. In 1806 English forces defeated the Dutch settlers and claimed the Cape of Good Hope as a British territory.[45]

The result of these occupations was the initial adoption of Roman Dutch law which, as it turned out did not cater for all the requirements of a society that was developing around the nineteenth century. It had therefore become necessary to resort to legislative innovation, which was often based on laws of England and interpreted in accordance with English precedent. In this way, significant aspects of English commercial law including company and trust law became established as part of the local law of South Africa.

Although in recent times, law reformers have either adapted or refined company law to better address the needs of the local South African

42 JSE Debt Listings Requirements. https://www.jse.co.za/content/JSERulesPoliciesandRegulationItems/JSE%20Debt%20Listings%20Requirements%20Service%20Issue%2025.pdf. (last visited 13 June 2019).

43 Hilary Joffe Sunday Times: JSE Proposals Seek to tighten Bond Market Listing Requirements. http://futuregrowth.co.za/newsroom/jse-proposals-seek-to-tighten-bond-market-listing-rules/ (last visited 13 June 2019).

44 South African History Online: The Union of South Africa 1910. https://www.sahistory.org.za/topic/union-south-africa-1910 (last visited 13 June 2019). Eight years after the end of the Boer War, on 31 May 1910, the Treaty of Vereeniging was concluded with the English colonial power. In terms of the treaty, South Africa became a Union thus achieving self-determination.

45 Amanda Barratt and Pamela Snyman, update by Salona Lutchman: Researching South African Law. http://www.nyulawglobal.org/globalex/South_Africa1.html (last visited 13 June 2019).

society, English precedent and, to an increasing extent, the precedents of other former English colonies including Canada, Australia, India and Hong Kong remain persuasive.[46]

(b) For comparative purposes, reference is made to the Financial Services Authority (FSA), previously the Securities and Investment Board, which was regulated in terms of the Financial Services and Markets Act 2000, an Act of the Parliament of the United Kingdom. The FSA was authorised to carry out the mandate of a regulator for insurance, investment business and banking. The creation of the FSA had brought 9 regulators together under one umbrella and therefore exercised a unitary model of regulation. By comparison the FSB SA, now FSCA, was established in terms of the Financial Services Board Act 97 of 1990 to regulate nonbanking financial services.[47] The FSB, in the same way as the FSA was established as a unitary regulator but without jurisdiction over banking.

At the time that the FSA was established, the Bank of England was still endeavouring to come to terms with the collapse of Barings which had occurred 2 years earlier. The FSA came in for a lot of criticism in the aftermath of the GFC. It was regarded as having failed to restrain the banks primarily due to its "light touch" approach to regulation. It was accused of not noticing that Northern Rock had been built on shaky foundations and that it could easily run out of liquid resources. It was also accused of failing to prevent the takeover of ABN Amro by the Royal Bank of Scotland just as the credit crunch was setting in during late 2007. Consequently, the FSA was split into two separate regulators namely a Prudential Regulatory Authority ("PRA") a subsidiary of the Bank of England to ensure that banks had sufficient capital and liquidity and the Financial Conduct Authority (FCA) whose main focus was to be market conduct regulation with the protection of investors at its core.[48]

Always keen watchers of regulatory developments in the United Kingdom, policymakers in South Africa felt constrained to examine their own financial services regulatory framework. The move from the FSA to the FCA in the United Kingdom was closely observed, in particular the

46 The Companies Act 71 of 2008, which was influenced significantly by the experience of the Canadian Consultants, contains significant revisions to previous editions of the Companies Act.

47 "Financial service" is defined as the financial service carried out by institutions including retirement funds, insurance companies, collective investment schemes and stock exchanges. Section 1 as read with section 3 Financial Services Board Act.

48 Jill Treanor: "Farewell to the FSA – and the Bleak Legacy of the Light-Touch Regulator". https://www.theguardian.com/business/2013/mar/24/farewell-fsa-bleak-legacy-light-touch-regulator (last visited 13 June 2019).

creation of the PRA and the FCA which had elements of a Twin Peaks model. It should be noted, however, that other than the corporate failures described under the discussion in the context of non systemic effects of the GFC on the stock market in South Africa, there were no systemic failures in the securities sector in South Africa.

Despite the absence of demonstrable systemic failures in the securities sector, the policymakers in South Africa nevertheless felt the need to embark on an extensive review of the securities regulatory framework. The following statement is to be found in the Redbook:

> This document provides a comprehensive review of the key challenges facing the financial sector, and proposes a roadmap to deal with the challenges it presents government's vision of how to reshape the sector in order to address these challenges, and sets out the policy priorities of government over the next five years.[49]

(c) A commentator, in an opinion piece which has resonance with the author,[50] opined that the debate on reform in South Africa

> is framed in such a way that South Africa must choose among three things: doing nothing, a single regulator or the twin peaks model.

The commentator argues that South Africa should not fall into this trap of having to choose between a single regulator or twin peaks models. In his view, South Africa should ensure that there is a legal framework that will promote coordination of regulatory policy, cooperation on enforcement matters and the sharing of information between two regulators or within a regulator. The commentator is not convinced by NT's main reasons for moving towards twin peaks i.e. "that it would be less disruptive" and that it is "the global trend." Indeed, the commentator argues, correctly in the author's view, that while many countries had reformed their regulatory frameworks in response to lessons emanating from the GFC, it would be an overstatement to attribute this to a global shift towards twin peaks. In reality, only two countries, the UK and Canada, adopted twin peaks under pressure from the aftermath of the crisis.[51]

---

49 Redbook, supra page 4.

50 Mtende Mhango "Approach with care when considering twin peaks." https://www.iol.co.za/business-report/opinion/approach-with-care-when-considering-twin-peaks-1656994 (last visited 13 June 2019).

51 Ibid.

Australia and Netherlands had adopted twin peaks before the crisis. Australia adopted this model in 1998 in accordance with the recommendations of the Wallis Inquiry of 1996. The Netherlands adopted twin peaks out of a desire to reduce the number of its financial regulators and also the influence of the broader regulatory changes in the EU.[52]

In short, the adoption of twin peaks by just 2 countries (UK and Canada) after the financial crisis could not reasonably be regarded as representing a global shift.[53]

Predictably, policy makers in South Africa beat a path to the UK, study tours were undertaken and UK based consultants engaged.[54] Tours to the Netherlands and Australia were also undertaken. Ultimately, guidance from the Australian and Netherlands models on the structural reforms, rather than investor protection issues which remained heavily influenced by the UK experience, was preferred on the basis that they were "generally held to have had a good (global financial) crisis."[55] The influence of these two countries in the formulation and development of the twin peaks model of regulation in South Africa is evident.

7 *Policy Developments – South Africa*

To recap, the key policy documents which were produced for the purposes of regulatory reform in the financial sector, specifically the securities sector are the "A Safer Financial Sector to serve South Africa better (the Redbook)",[56] "Implementing a Twin Peaks Model of Financial Regulation in South Africa" published in February 2013[57] and "Twin Peaks in South Africa" published in December 2014.[58] These documents are discussed further below. Much of the focus of these documents was on the retail aspect of financial services (insurance, pensions and aspects of banking) and almost only a passing reference to non-retail aspects of capital markets and securities.

---

52 Ibid.

53 Ibid. Another concern the author had at the time was the absence of any evident interrogation of the status quo in the securities and capital markets sector or a needs analysis justifying the reforms to follow.

54 Their role in the adoption of a UK influenced Treating Customers Fairly framework and the direction of the Retail Distribution Review, for instance, is considerable.

55 National Treasury: Implementing a Twin Peaks Model of Financial Regulation in South Africa 1 February 2013, page 23. http://www.treasury.gov.za/twinpeaks/20131211%20-%20Item%203%20Roadmap.pdf (last visited 3 June 2019).

56 Supra.

57 "Implementing a twin peaks model of financial regulation in South Africa" 1 February 2013, supra.

58 National Treasury: https://old.juta.co.za/media/filestore/2015/03/2014_12_12_Response_document.pdf. (last visited 13 June 2019).

(a) A Safer Financial Sector to Serve South Africa Better (Redbook). This document sets forth 4 policy priorities:
   i. Financial Stability. In furtherance of this priority a number of initiatives were identified including
      – The establishment of a "Financial Stability Oversight Committee" comprising the SARB, the FSB (now FSCA) and the NT;[59]
      – The establishment of a "Council of Financial Regulators" intended to provide interagency coordination amongst regulators on issues of legislation, enforcement and market conduct. Standard setters such as the Independent Regulatory Board of Auditors (IRBA) would also be included;[60]
      – Improved Banking and Financial Crisis Resolution Frameworks. (Ongoing work on this initiative focused on improving interagency coordination and finalising a comprehensive joint review of the crisis contingency framework);[61]
      – International Peer-Review. (As a member of the G20 Group of Nations, South Africa committed itself to international peer-review. During 2010 the IMF and the World Bank jointly assessed South Africa's compliance with international regulatory best practice in banking, insurance and securities regulation.[62] A further assessment was carried out during 2015).
   ii. Consumer protection and market conduct. The observation had been made that the South African financial sector was characterised by high and opaque fees including the unfair treatment of customers. It was also observed that, savings instruments tended to be limited, expensive and inappropriate. In addition, the difficulty for small and medium-sized enterprises to access credit was noted. To address these challenges the following proposals were made:
      – The creation of a retail banking services market conduct regulator in the FSCA to focus on issues of market structure and bank costs and to work with the National Credit Regulator Banking Services to address the regulation of the extension of credit;[63] and

---

59 Supra Redbook, page 5.
60 Supra Redbook, page 5.
61 Supra Redbook, page 6.
62 Supra Redbook, page 6.
63 The FCA in June 2018 published a wide ranging review of its retail banking sector. On 30 April 2019, the FSCA published a statement supporting a draft conduct standard for banks.

- The implementation of a comprehensive treating customers fairly initiative "with clear principles for market conduct backed by rules."[64]

iii. Expansion of access to financial services through financial inclusion. The main focus of this priority is the improvement of access to financial services for the poor, vulnerable and those living in rural communities. Also, the implementation of the transformation objectives of the Financial Sector Charter was intended to facilitate the transformation and the promotion of broad based Black Economic Empowerment.[65]

iv. Combating Financial Crime. The crimes contemplated under this priority include the "stealing of trust" and beneficiary funds, money laundering and the burgeoning world-wide problem of terrorist financing.[66]

(b) Implementing a Twin Peaks Model of Financial Regulation in South Africa. The intention was for this document to provide more detailed proposals for implementing the initiatives identified in the Redbook, in the process setting out the approach to prudential (the maintenance and enhancement of the safety and soundness of regulated institutions) and market conduct (the protection of consumers of financial services and the promotion of confidence in the South African financial system) regulation.[67] This document confirmed the decision to implement the twin peaks model of financial services regulation. The priorities of this document are presented in 7 distinct chapters:

i. Enhancement of the 4 objectives identified in the Redbook.[68] In addition, the intention was to ensure that the regulatory and supervisory framework was

transparent; comprehensive and consistent; appropriate, intensive and intrusive; outcomes based; risk-based and proportional; pre-emptive and proactive; a credible deterrent to

64 Supra, Redbook page 6.

65 Supra, Redbook page 7. Black Economic Empowerment is an overarching policy implemented by government for the purposes of redistributing wealth and redressing the inequities of the past.

66 Supra, Redbook page 7. The Fidentia (Widows and Orphans) case is relevant under this initiative.

67 Implementing a Twin Peaks Model of Financial Regulation in South Africa. Supra, page 6.

68 Financial Stability Consumer, Protection and Market Conduct, Financial Inclusion and Combating Financial Crime.

non-compliance with prescribed standards; and aligned with applicable international standards.[69]

In order to realise these principles, an appropriate licensing process would be implemented including a high standard for the determination of fitness and propriety.

ii. Governance and Accountability Framework. This priority takes cognizance of the need for regulators to have operational independence, thus allowing them to perform their duties impartially.

iii. Strengthening Financial Stability Oversight. Under this priority the Financial Stability Oversight Committee would be given legislative backing in order to coordinate efforts to maintain financial stability and limit risk. In the securities sector, the licensing regime for certain financial market infrastructures would provide for better monitoring and mitigation of the risks posed by over-the-counter derivative instruments.[70]

iv. Prudential Regulation and Supervision. This priority sets out the various steps to be taken by the prudential regulator to enable it to execute its mandate.[71]

v. Market Conduct Regulation and Supervision. This priority sets out the tools that would be available to the market conduct regulator to enable it to execute its mandate including ad hoc on-site visits and information requests, "mystery shopper" techniques and consumer and industry surveys.[72]

vi. Crisis Management and Resolution. The priority under this head is to ensure that there are mechanisms in place to deal with disruptions which may threaten financial stability including a resolution framework. Stability in these circumstances applies to all elements of the financial system which are systemically significant and could include banks, non-bank financial institutions, major participants or exposures in initial markets.[73]

vii. Enforcement. Various approaches contemplated for the effective implementation of Twin Peaks include summary administrative penalties, referrals to an administrative forum and criminal

69 Implementing a Twin Peaks Model of Financial Regulation in South Africa. Supra, pages 6 and 7.

70 Supra, pages 9 and 10. The financial market infrastructures contemplated are central counterparties and trade Repositories.

71 Supra, page 10.

72 Supra, page 11.

73 Supra, page 11.

prosecution. Supervisory actions include the suspension or withdrawal of licences and approvals as well as the issuing of orders to take or cease particular actions and departments.[74]

(c) Twin Peaks in South Africa.[75] This is the last in the trilogy of policy papers which accompanied the Financial Sector Regulation Bill which became the Financial Sector Regulation Act 9 of 1917 (FSRA) on 18 April 2018.

i. The main purpose of this paper was to pave the way towards the implementation of the twin peaks model of regulation for financial services. The difficulty of moving from the sectoral approach to "functional" regulation is demonstrated by the fact that work on the roadmap to reform commenced in 2008 in the throes of the GFC and was only completed in April 2018 with the promulgation of the FSRA. In other words, it took almost 10 years to get to this point. In the circumstances the implementation of Twin Peaks and other reforms can only be a gradual process in view of the amount of work still to be done.

ii. Now that the FSRA has been promulgated, what still remains to be done is to grant to the 2 authorities (Prudential and Market Conduct) the necessary powers to appropriately regulate and supervise financial institutions from their first day of operation. These powers would be in addition to those provided in the existing sectoral law and are intended to ensure that the authorities have the required tools to perform effectively without being limited by gaps in their existing sectoral roles.[76] This process takes cognizance of the shortcomings in existing sectoral laws and allows for an overlay of additional powers.

iii. In the final phase, the reforms will be more far-reaching as the legal frameworks for prudential and market conduct regulation, will be streamlined with the intention of "improving them". This actually entails repealing sectoral legislation and introducing new legislation and licensing procedures. The following is an indication of the way forward for the "pillars" of the regulatory framework:

- Licensing: financial sector laws[77] will be repealed and replaced. Licensing will be in terms of a single prudential and a single market conduct law;

74 Supra, page 12.

75 National treasury: Twin Peaks in South Africa. https://juta.co.za/media/filestore/2015/03/2014_12_12_Response_document.pdf (last visited 13 June 2019).

76 Ibid., page 6.

77 As defined in section 1 FSRA.

- Setting standards and regulatory requirements (subordinate legislation): the intention is to eventually phase out the existing range of subordinate legislation and to replace it with standards.[78] In the target framework, all requirements issued by the authorities will be in terms of standards. The new standardised system will differentiate between actions of general application and actions of specific application. In the case of actions of general application, a system of primary legislation, regulations, standards, interpretation notes and guidance notes is proposed. In the case of actions of specific application, a system of administrative actions is proposed;
- Supervision, including collecting information and inspections: Provisions in financial sector laws will be repealed and replaced with provisions in prudential law and market conduct law respectively:
  - Administrative actions, including enforcement actions: provisions in financial sector laws are to be repealed. Note that the FSRA includes powers to investigate potential wrongdoing, to fine, and to enter into enforceable undertakings.[79]
  - Self Regulatory Organisation (SRO) Review. The SRO model of regulation has been in existence for some considerable time. For instance, at the time that Congress in the US created the Securities and Exchange Commission (SEC) in 1934, stock exchanges, as private associations, had been regulating their members for up to 140 years. Rather than displacing the system of self-regulation, Congress superimposed the SEC on the exchanges as an additional level of regulation. As a consequence, exchanges have maintained and enforced a large body of rules for the conduct of their members. These rules fall into two categories namely rules relating to transactions on the particular exchanges and rules relating to internal operations of the member firms and their dealings with their customers.[80] The situation is similar in South Africa. The JSE was formed in 1887 during the first South African gold rush.[81]

78 When one considers the definition of "standard" and "conduct standard" in section 1 and 106 of the FSRA, the distinction between standards and subordinate legislation is not clear.

79 Ibid. pages 8–10.

80 Securities Regulation in a Nutshell, 10th edition, ISBN: 978-0-314-18798-7.

81 African Markets: About the Johannesburg Stock Exchange. https://www.african-markets.com/en/stock-markets/jse/about (last visited 13 June 2019).

The FSB SA was established only in 1991 to create an independent body to supervise and regulate the non-banking financial services industry including the only existing exchange at the time.[82] The SRO model has various permutations including a strong SRO and co-regulator model. Over the years, the JSE developed a strong SRO model whereby it has had primary responsibility for the regulation of its listed entities and its members. The FSCA (and previously the FSB SA) has direct contact with the JSE's listed entities and members only in exceptional circumstances.[83]

As part of the cluster of regulatory issues arising in the course of regulatory reform, NT took the opportunity to address the question of whether or not a strong SRO model as embodied in the structure of the JSE and the sole central securities depository, STRATE (Pty) Limited was appropriate for the South African capital markets. The UK for instance has moved away from the strong SRO model. The requirement now in the UK is for applications for admission to the official list on the Main Market to be submitted to FCA, acting through the UK Listing Authority (UKLA), in the first instance. Subsequently an application is required to be submitted to the London Stock Exchange for admission of securities to trading. The FCA as the primary regulator determines the criteria governing listing and publishes rules and regulations for listed companies.[84]

In South Africa where the strong SRO model still pertains, a licensed exchange is required, inter-alia, to have made arrangements for the "efficient and effective monitoring of compliance by issuers of securities listed on the exchange with the exchange's listings requirements."[85] In addition, the listings requirements of the exchange are required to prescribe:

- the manner in which securities may be listed or removed from the list or in which trading in securities may be suspended;

82 Financial Sector Conduct Authority: About the FSB. www.fsca.co.za (last visited 13 June 2019).

83 Sections 94–96 Financial Markets Act 19 of 2012.

84 David Tricot and Adam M. Howard, Skadden, Arps, Slate, Meagher: Initial Public Offerings Law Review: https://www.skadden.com/-/media/files/publications/2017/06/united_kingdom_ipo.pdf (last visited 13 June 2019).

85 Section 8 (1) (e) FMA: requirements applicable to … (a) licensed exchange.

– requirements with which issuers of securities must comply[86]
Clearly, the FCA through the UK Listing Authority, has greater direct involvement in the listings process than the FSB SA (now FSCA) which monitors and supervises the JSE in the exercise of the listings authority accorded to it by the FMA.

The question faced by the NT therefore, was whether the current SRO model needed to be reviewed and whether the FSB SA (now FSCA) should have a more direct involvement in the listings process. After consultation, the NT concluded that the "SRO model and South Africa's capital markets have proved resilient over recent years of financial sector instability". In the circumstances, no changes were proposed to the SRO model as applied in South Africa, although potential weaknesses in the existing structure were recognised, particularly with respect to conflicts of interest and engagement processes. Accordingly, certain amendments were proposed and subsequently made to the relevant sections of the FMA.[87] Another reason for the policymakers' reluctance to move away from the relative assurance of the SRO model, would have been the dearth of relevant skills and expertise within the regulator to enable it to assume a similar role to the UKLA. At this stage, the FSCA has no involvement in the listings process or the filing and scrutiny of annual financial statements except in reported cases of market abuse. The skills deficit at the FSCA is exacerbated by resource constraints.

86 Section 11 (a) and (b) FMA: Listing of Securities. This section sets out additional requirements for the listing of securities.

87 Explanatory Memorandum on the Financial Markets Bill 2012, April 2012: Treasury Comments on issues Raised During the Consultation Period for the Financial Markets Bill. http://www.treasury.gov.za/legislation/bills/2012/FMB/FMB%20Explanatory%20Memorandum.pdf. (last visited 13 June 2019). The issue of SROs has been revisited and not really taken any further in the 2018 Financial Markets Review, where the following recommendations (number 38) is made: "It is recommended that the SRO model be retained where appropriate. It is further recommended that SROs' delegation of regulatory authority be revisited to maximise the benefits of self-regulation and limit its disadvantages (mainly conflicts of interest)." See NT, South African Reserve Bank and FSCA: 2018 Financial Markets Review. http://www.treasury.gov.za/publications/other/2018_FMR_07.pdf (last visited 13 June 2019).

8 *Legislative Changes*

In the reform process, changes or additions were made to the following pieces of legislation: FMA, CRSA, CISCA and Financial Intelligence Centre Act 35 of 2001 (FICA).[88] Many of the changes are incorporated by reference in the FSRA. The objectives of the changes in these pieces of legislation will be highlighted below and specific provisions will be discussed further in the regulation section to follow.

(a) FMA: Notable objectives in this Act, which replaced the SSA, include:
   i. ensuring that the South African financial markets are fair, efficient and transparent;[89]
   ii. increasing confidence in the South African financial markets by requiring securities services to be provided in a fair, efficient and transparent manner, in addition contributing to the maintenance of a stable national market environment;[90]
   iii. reducing systemic risk;[91] and
   iv. promoting international and domestic competitiveness of South African financial markets and securities services.[92]

   The objectives of the FMA should be viewed in the context of the policy considerations set out is section 2 (Periodic Review).

   In addition to the foregoing generic enhancements to the FMA, a specific development is the introduction of the electronic trading platform (ETP) for Government Bonds. The background to this development goes back to the acquisition of the Bond Exchange of South Africa by the JSE during 2009. One of the conditions for the approval of this acquisition was the requirement for the JSE to develop an interest rate strategy in the context of the sovereign bond market to support transparency, trading and liquidity. Protracted consultations amongst the NT, other regulators and the industry followed. The International Bank for Reconstruction and Development (World Bank) provided advisory services. Eventually on 19 September 2014, the NT announced that it would be implementing an ETP

88 The effects of the FICA Act are incidental to the operations of capital markets, and are included for the sake of completeness.

89 FMA section 2 (a).

90 FMA section 2 (b).

91 FMA section 2 (d). This is in line with new IOSCO principle 6: "The Regulator should have or contribute to a process to monitor, mitigate and manage systemic risk, appropriate to its mandate."

92 FMA section 2 (e).

for the primary dealers (PDs) so that their secondary market quoting obligations under the "Primary Dealer" contract[93] with the NT would need to be satisfied on the ETP. The NT explained that the primary reason for this decision was the need to enhance transparency within the South African Bond Market and to enable the NT to more accurately monitor the activities of the PDs.[94] On 16 July 2018, FSCA approved amendments to the relevant JSE Rules thereby operationalising the ETP.[95] It is still early to comment on the success or otherwise of the ETP initiative which is focused on the central order book and how it will affect the PDs who have previously conducted their dealings over the counter.

(b) CRSA: This is a new Act which is in line with IOSCO's Principle 22.[96] Key objects of the CRSA are to:

i. ensure responsible and accountable credit rating agencies;[97]
ii. protect the integrity, transparency and reliability of the credit rating process and credit ratings;[98]
iii. improve investor protection;[99]
iv. improve the fairness, efficiency and transparency of financial markets;[100] and
v. reduce systemic risk.

---

93 For a sample of this periodically announced obligation, see NT: Secondary Market Making Obligation on the R2023 (7.75 per cent: 2023) by Primary Dealers In Fixed Rate Government Bonds of the Republic of South Africa. http://www.treasury.gov.za/comm_media/press/2012/2012090501.pdf (last visited 13 June 2019).

94 NT: MEDIA STATEMENT Electronic Trading Platform for RSA Government Bonds. http://www.treasury.gov.za/comm_media/press/2014/2104091902%20-%20Media%20Statement%20ETP%20for%20RSA%20Government%20Bonds.pdf (last visited 13 June 2019).

95 SA Government Gazette: Financial Markets Act: Amendments: JSE Bond Electronic Trading Platform Rules. https://www.gov.za/sites/default/files/41773_bn91.pdf (last visited 13 June 2019).

96 "Credit rating agencies should be subject to adequate levels of oversight. The regulatory system should ensure that credit rating agencies whose ratings are used for regulatory purposes are subject to registration and ongoing supervision." Credit rating agencies are very active in the rating of various debt instruments in South Africa.

97 CRSA section 2 (a).

98 CRSA section 2 (b). In the aftermath of the GFC, the role of credit rating agencies came under scrutiny, in particular the remuneration model which was not designed to prevent conflicts of interest.

99 CRSA section 2 (c).

100 CRSA section 2 (d).

Areas of this act which may in future come under review, include the restrictive definition of "credit rating services."[101] As this definition is currently crafted, the argument has been put forward that opinions rather than ratings are not regulated. In a recent case before the Hong Kong Final Court Appeal, that particular issue was considered in the context of an allegation of misconduct. The judgment is instructive.[102]

(c) CISCA: The most significant developments in the framework provided for by this Act are with respect to hedge funds, real estate investment trusts and advertising, marketing and disclosure.

i. Hedge funds have been brought into the regulatory framework in line with IOSCO Principle 28.[103] The challenge faced by policymakers and regulators in South Africa initially, was how to extend the regulatory framework to hedge funds which had hitherto been unregulated. Cognizance was taken of the reality that hedge funds like collective investment schemes are pooled funds. A practical decision was therefore taken to extend the reach of CISCA to include hedge funds. The business of a hedge fund was declared to be a collective investment scheme in terms of section 63 (1) of CISCA.[104] The regulations dealing with hedge funds distinguish between a qualified investor fund[105] in which only a qualified investor[106] can invest and a retail investor fund in which any investor may

---

101 CRSA section 1: "credit rating services means data and information analysis, evaluation, approval, issuing or review, for the purposes of credit ratings." From this definition, it has been argued by credit rating agencies that "opinions" are not covered.

102 Moody's Investors Services Hong Kong Limited v Securities and Futures Commission [2018] HKCFA 42. The question for decision had been whether a report raising, inter alia, corporate governance concerns at 61 Chinese companies was "an act or omission relating to the carrying on of any regulated activity for which a person is licensed or registered which in the opinion of the Commission, is or is likely to be prejudicial to the interest of the investing public or to the public interest." Section 193 (1) (d) of Securities and Futures Ordinance (Cap 571).

103 "Regulation should ensure that hedge funds and/or hedge funds managers/advisers are subject to appropriate oversight."

104 GN 141 of 25 February 2015: Declaration of hedge fund business As a Collective Investment Scheme (Government Gazette No. 38503).

105 CISCA section 3.

106 Section 1 CISCA Hedge Funds Regulations: "qualified investor" means any person who invests a minimum amount of R 1 million per hedge fund, and who (a) has demonstrable knowledge and experience in financial and business matters which would enable the investor to assess merits and risks of a hedge fund investment; or (b) has appointed a financial services provider who has demonstrable knowledge and experience to advise the investor regarding the merits and risks of a hedge fund investment.

invest.[107] These changes to CISCA did not only extend the regulatory perimeter to hedge funds. They also increased investment options for both qualified and retail investors.

ii. Real estate investment trusts. For many years tradeable investment in the property sector in South Africa was in the form of property loan stock companies (PLSs) and collective investment schemes in property (CISPs). Although PLSs did not enjoy the same tax concessions which were available to CISPs, they had other advantages such as the ability to manage their property portfolios within the same group unlike CISPs. As part of engagements between policymakers and industry over a period of time, a document entitled "Reforming the Listed Property Sector in South Africa" was prepared and utilised as the basis for public consultation.[108] At the conclusion of the consultation process, the Taxation Laws Amendment Act, 2012 (Act No. 22 of 2012)[109] was passed. This Amendment Act introduced a tax dispensation for South African REITs which has had the effect of creating tax parity between the two types of property investment vehicles (PLSs and CISPs). In the circumstances, it was necessary for the FSB SA, the regulator at the time, to introduce a process in terms of which CISPs could be converted to corporate REITs. After conversion, CISPs no longer fell within the regulatory ambit of CISCA or the Registrar of CISs.[110] Whether a proposed listed property investment is structured as a REIT or CISP, it is still required to comply with the requirements of the exchange on which it lists.[111]

iii. Advertising, Marketing and Information Disclosure Requirements for CISs.[112] The objectives of this notice were stated as being to:

---

107 Section 1 CISCA.

108 http://www.treasury.gov.za/publicpercent20comments/REITSpercent20discussionpercent20document.pdf (last visited 13 June 2019).

109 https://www.sars.gov.za/AllDocs/LegalDoclib/AmendActs/LAPD-LPrim-AA-2012-03%20-%20Taxation%20Laws%20Amendment%20Act%202012.pdf (last visited 13 June 2019).

110 Financial Services Board Notice 42 of 2014, Collective Investment Schemes Control Act, 2002: Conditions for the Winding up of a Collective Investment Scheme in Property under Certain Circumstances.

111 JSE Listings Requirements, Section 13: Property Entities. Over the past 6 years "the number of REITs listed on the JSE has increased over the period from less than 30 to over 50" See Fin24: Why it makes sense to invest in REITs. https://www.fin24.com/Economy/why-it-makes-sense-to-invest-in-reits-20180328.

112 Financial Services Board Notice 92 of 2014, Collective Investment Schemes Control Act, 2002. https://www.fsb.co.za/Departments/cis/Documents/Board%20Notice%2092%20of%202014.pdf.

- provide for the advertising and marketing of products in a manner which ensures that investors base their investment decisions on full, accurate and comprehensive information;
- protect investors from deceptive, misleading, unfair or fraudulent conduct by managers through advertising and marketing material;
- promote the fair treatment of investors;
- encourage fair competition amongst managers;
- promote the use of plain and understandable language by managers in respect of any information provided or displayed to investors;[113]
- ensure alignment with relevant international information disclosure standards and practices;
- encourage the use of suitable disclosures for the intended target market; and
- determine the manner in which managers are required to lodge advertising and marketing material.[114]

The changes under this section detail the requirements for disclosure with an emphasis on transparency, suitability and fairness and are, for comparative purposes, substantially consistent with the thrust of the MiFID 2 Supervisory briefing on suitability.[115]

(d) FSRA. This is the first of a series of intended legislative additions and changes designed to facilitate the introduction and transition to the twin peaks model of regulation.[116] The FSRA made significant changes to the financial services regulatory landscape in South Africa. It covers the SARB as the prudential regulator, and FSCA as the market conduct regulator. Again, in line with the policy considerations in section 2 (Periodic Review) FSCA's objectives in terms of the FSRA are to:

---

113 The requirement for a Key Investor Information Document emphasises simplicity and plain language and is very different to the nature and content of a prospectus, the standard offer document in initial public offerings.

114 Section 2 Financial Services Board Notice 92 of 2014, Collective Investment Schemes Control Act, 2002.

115 ESMA publishes MiFID II Supervisor Briefing on Suitability. https://www.esma.europa.eu/press-news/esma-news/esma-publishes-mifid-ii-supervisory-briefing-suitability (last visited 13 June 2019).

116 FSB newsletter: "A new playing field with the introduction of FSCA … The FSRA will … operate as an 'overlay' over the existing sectoral laws. This status quo will remain until such time that the Conduct of Financial Institutions Act (COFI is in place and all current licences are converted to a market conduct licence". See Jonathan Fourie: A New Playing Field with the Introduction of the FSCA. http://www.fia.org.za/blog/a-new-playing-field-with-the-introduction-of-the-fsca/ (last visited 13 June 2019).

i. enhance and support the efficiency and integrity of financial markets;[117]
ii. protect financial customers by promoting their fair treatment by financial institutions and providing them as well as potential financial customers with financial education programs. There is also a requirement to promote financial literacy and the ability of financial customers and potential financial customers to make sound financial decisions;[118] and
iii. assist in maintaining financial stability[119]

In place of an executive officer and deputy executive officers provided for in the Financial Services Board Act No. 97 of 1990, the management of FSCA is now assigned to a commissioner and deputy commissioners.[120]

---

117 FSRA section 57 (a).

118 FSRA section 57 (b).

119 FSRA section 57 (c).

120 FRSA section 61. Around the time that the decision was taken to adopt the twin peaks model of financial regulation with particular attention being paid to the Australian model, the consulting firm Promontory which at one point had as advisors such luminaries as Mary Shapiro, former chair of the US Securities and Exchange Commission, was engaged to assist with the transition. In an interesting variation to the governance structure currently in effect in Australia where the operational direction of the Australian Securities and Investment Commission is assigned to 5 full-time commissioners including the chair, the management of FSCA as proposed in the first draft of the Financial Sector Regulation Bill and retained in the final FSRA is assigned to the Commissioner and between 2 and 4 **deputy** commissioners. Apparently, all levels of oversight and management report into the Commissioner. This curious governance set up is different even to the US Securities and Exchange Commission where, in a similar setup to Australia, the operational direction of the SEC is assigned to 5 commissioners, of whom one is the chair. See ASIC: How We Operate. https://asic.gov.au/about-asic/what-we-do/how-we-operate/ (last visited 13 June 2019). For the US SEC see https://www.sec.gov/Article/about-commissioners.html (current SEC Commissioners) (last visited 13 June 2019). Shortly after the promulgation of the Dodd-Frank Act (DFA) in the US, the author witnessed, with his capital markets team, a live debate at the Commodities and Futures Exchange Commission which has a similar commission structure to the SEC. The debate was about the implementation of the DFA. (SA's interest in the debate was in view of the extra-territorial effects of the DFA on "swap-dealers" operating in SA, a situation previously raised with the chairman of the CFTC Gary Gensler by the author when both were members of the IOSCO board). In view of the equal status of the chairman Gary Gensler and a dissenting commissioner Scott O'Malia, the debate was robust and maybe a bit irreverent. (Scott O'Malia is now the head of the International Swap Dealers Association). During the consultation process on the FSRA, reservations were expressed about the proposed transfer of concentration of power from the executive officer of the FSB SA to the Commissioner. Optically, when compared to the situation at both ASIC in Australia and the SEC United States, the position of the Commissioner in South Africa was not designed to be collegial. Engagement by a deputy executive officer with the executive officer (read deputy commissioner and

Invitations to apply for the posts of Commissioner and deputy commissioners were advertised early in 2018. Applications closed on 21 May 2018.[121] As at the date of this work (May 2019) no appointments have been made. In the meantime and:

> as a transitional measure and to ensure a seamless transition to the FSCA, the Minister has determined that the current FSB Executive Committee will stay on to assist with the creation of the FSCA and dis-establishment of the FSB. The Minister has further determined that the Chairperson of the current FSB Board … will be caretaking i.e. acting as the FSCA Commissioner until the new Commissioner is appointed.[122]

In an unexpected development and prior to the appointment of the commissioner and deputy commissioners, members of the transitional management committee have been appointed divisional executives in key positions at the FSCA including the all important regulatory strategy.[123] The perception of self-interest and even conflict may be difficult to counter. The new executive, when it is eventually appointed, could find itself in an invidious, even compromised position, in the event that it does not share the same vision as the oldguard. In furtherance of this perception, the Regulatory Strategy of the FSCA for the period October 2018 to September 2021 was published in October 2018.[124]

(e) FICA. South Africa is a member of the Financial Action Task Force (FATF), an international body that works with financial institutions to combat financial crime. It was after South Africa joined the FATF in 2003 that FICA, which regulates financial institutions was adopted.[125] The

---

commissioner) in the same way O'Malia confronted Gensler, would surely not have had a collegial result.

121 NT: Commissioner and Deputy Commissioners of the Financial Sector Conduct Authority Pretoria. http://www.treasury.gov.za/careers/Commissioner%20and%20Deputy%20of%20the%20Financial%20Sector%20Conduct%20Authority.pdf (last visited 13 June 2019).

122 FSCA: Meet the Commissioners. https://www.fsca.co.za/Pages/Commissioners.aspx. (last visited 13 June 2019). See next footnote dealing with the appointment of divisional executives. The title of the announcement in the current footnote "Meet the Commissioners" curiously refers to the divisional executives.

123 Money Marketing: FSCA Commissioner appoints Divisional Executives. https://www.moneymarketing.co.za/fsca-commissioner-appoints-divisional-executives/ (last visited 13 June 2019).

124 FSCA Strategy 2018. https://www.fsca.co.za/Documents/FSCA_Strategy_2018.pdf (last visited 13 June 2019).

125 Ra'eesa Pather: "Everything You Need to Know about the FIC Amendment Bill." https://mg.co.za/article/2017-01-31-crib-notes-everything-you-need-to-know-about-the-fic-amendment-bill/ (last visited 13 June 2019).

principal objective of the FICA is to assist in the identification of the proceeds of unlawful activities and the combating of money laundering activities as well as the financing of terrorist and related activities.[126] FICA was recently amended in order to address shortcomings identified during an assessment by FATF. It now contains stringent requirements regarding, inter-alia, understanding and obtaining information about a business relationship with a prospective client,[127] additional due diligence measures relating to legal persons, trusts and partnerships[128] and the requirement to conduct ongoing due diligence in accordance with its "Risk Management and Compliance Programme".[129] In respect of a business relationship, due diligence is required to include an enquiry into the source of funds and the background and purpose of complex and unusual large transactions which have no apparent business or lawful purpose.[130] In addition, where a prospective client is a foreign prominent public official,[131] the accountable institution[132] must obtain senior management approval in order to establish the business relationship, take reasonable measures to establish the source of wealth and source of funds of the client and conduct enhanced ongoing monitoring

126 Section 3 FICA.

127 Section 21A FICA.

128 Section 21B FICA.

129 Section 42 FICA. The essence of the requirement for a Risk Management and Compliance programme, is that it must enable the accountable institution to identify; assess; monitor; mitigate and manage the risk contemplated. Authorised users of an exchange, managers of CISs and financial services providers authorised under FAIS are all accountable institutions (Schedule 1 FICA). The SARB and the FSCA are the designated supervisory bodies (Schedule 2 FICA). In addition to their duties as supervisory bodies, they are required to "generally assist and support each other in pursuing their objectives in terms of ... FICA." (Section 76 FSRA). Both the SARB and the FSCA are either in the process of implementing or consolidating the implementation of risk based supervision (RBS – discussed further under section B Supervision infra) in respect of their regulated entities. It is logical that they should extend RBS to the activities of their regulated entities as contemplated by FICA.

130 Section 21D FICA.

131 Defined in Schedule 3B of FICA as a head of state or head of a country or government; member of a foreign royal family; government minister or equivalent; politician or leader of a political party; senior judicial official; senior executive of a state owned corporation; or a high-ranking member of the military.

132 Defined in Schedule 1 to include attorneys, boards of executors or trust companies, estate agents, managers of CISs, banks, insurers, persons dealing in foreign currency, persons carrying on the business of lending money against the security of securities and financial services providers who are required to be authorised in terms of the Financial Advisory and Intermediary Services Act 37 of 2002, amongst other specified institutions.

of the business relationship.[133] In the case of a prospective client who is a domestic prominent influential person[134] again, the institution is required to carry out the same due diligence as for a foreign prominent public official.

The board of directors or the senior management of an accountable institution is required to ensure compliance by the institution and its employees with the provisions of FICA and its Risk Management and Compliance Programme.[135] Should the board of directors or senior management of the accountable institution fail to comply with this requirement they will be regarded as non-compliant and subject to administrative action.[136]

9 *Capital Markets Value Chain*

A discussion of regulation in the context of securities and capital markets can be facilitated by reference to a value chain which traces activity from product availability, intermediaries, trading platforms all the way through to settlement and payment as well as the reporting of data to trade repositories. This discussion of regulation will follow the sequence of securities, collective investment schemes, intermediaries, trading platforms, public offers, the Takeover Code, corporate governance and audit, trading and financial market infrastructures (clearinghouses, central securities depositories including settlement, payment systems including real-time gross payment and the role of the SARB).

(a) "Securities" which may be listed or unlisted are defined in the FMA to include:
   i. shares,[137] depositary receipts and other equivalent equities in public companies;
   ii. debentures and bonds issued by public companies, public state-owned enterprises, the SARB and the Government of the Republic of South Africa;
   iii. derivative instruments;
   iv. (debt) notes;

133 Section 21G FICA.

134 Defined in Schedule 3A as the President or Deputy President, a government minister or Deputy Minister, the Premier of the province, certain other politically connected figures and senior management of companies providing goods or services to an organ of state where the transactional value exceeds a prescribed amount.

135 Section 42A.

136 Section 61B. The process for administrative actions is set out in Section 45C.

137 Simply defined in the Companies Act 71 of 2008 as "one of the units into which the proprietary interest in a profit company is divided."

v. participating interests in CISs including units or any other form of participation in a foreign CIS approved in terms of CISCA; and
vi. instruments based on an index (exchange traded funds).[138]

Shares come in a number of different configurations. The most common form is the ordinary share where shareholders hold units of equal value and equal rights.[139] However, as the financing needs of an entity increase, the financing instruments can become more complex, and one can encounter several classes of ordinary shares. Most ordinary shares have voting rights, with one share carrying one vote. In the case where a company has different classes of shares, it is not unusual for there to be different voting rights attaching to the separate classes of shares.[140] As in the case of the US company Facebook and more recently Lyft, it is not unusual to encounter so-called founders shares which are designed to entrench control in the founders of the business, with other classes of shares being issued merely for financing purposes. Shares with differential voting rights such as N-ordinary shares have been used extensively in South Africa in the context of broad-based black economic empowerment.[141]

---

138 Section 1 FMA.

139 Equal rights, often referred to as "pari passu".

140 Facebook for instance has a dual-class structure. Class A shares, which trade under the ticker "FB" on public markets and have one vote per share, and Class B shares, which have 10 votes per share and is what company insiders own. The Class B shares don't trade on an exchange. Facebook recently announced that it would create a new "Class C" stock that would have the same economic rights as the current Class A and Class B shares but have no voting rights. See Myles Udland: "Facebook has a new class structure and Mark Zuckerberg is still in control". https://www.businessinsider.com/facebook-new-stock-structure-2016-4?IR=T (last visited 13 June 2019). Naspers Limited, a South African company has two classes of shares (a) N class ordinary shares, that have one vote per share and are listed on the JSE; and (b) Unlisted A class ordinary shares, that have one thousand votes per share, but have relatively insignificant economic participation. Dividends declared to A ordinary shareholders are equal to one-fifth of the dividends per share to which N ordinary shareholders are entitled. See Naspers: "The Naspers voting control structure ensures continued independence of the group". https://www.naspers.com/about/control-structure (last visited 13 June 2019).

141 "broad-based black economic empowerment (BBBEE)" means "the viable economic empowerment of all black people … through diverse but integrated socio-economic strategies that include, but are not limited to: increasing the number of black people that manage, own and control enterprises and productive assets; facilitating ownership and management of enterprises and productive assets by communities, workers, co-operatives and other collective enterprises; and investment in enterprises that are owned or managed by black people". Broad-Based Black Economic Empowerment Act 53 of 2003. The genuineness of BBBEE structures has recently been brought into question by

Shareholders may initially back a company with different classes of shares and actually be content with low voting shares as long as the company is performing. However low voting shares become problematic when the company's fortunes deteriorate and there is a strong perception that such deterioration is attributable to the actions or non-actions of management. In these circumstances, owing to the low voting impact of their aggregate shareholdings, they are unable to effect the necessary changes to management.

In addition to ordinary shares and low voting shares and N-shares, other configurations include preference shares with for instance, a fixed or variable dividend and also a conversion feature.

Debentures and bonds are both debt instruments which can be held privately or be listed on an exchange. They can also contain conversion rights into equity. A type of bond which is recommended by the Basel Committee on Banking Supervision in order to provide additional loss absorbency for banks is the contingent convertible bond.[142]

In South Africa, bonds are issued by Government, state owned enterprises and corporates.[143] These instruments can be accessed for investment on the JSE where they are publicly listed. Some of the instruments can be accessed over the counter.

Derivative instruments are those financial instruments which derive their existence and value from an underlying asset. Derivatives which are available for investment in South Africa on both public markets and over-the-counter include equity, agricultural, commodity, bond, interest rate and currency derivatives. Common equity derivatives include single stock futures which can be listed on an exchange and contracts for difference which are available over-the-counter. Single stock futures and contracts for difference, both carry a margin requirement as collateral for trading. During 2009, owing to a spate of defaults on single stock futures transactions, the JSE was compelled to tighten the rules on margin, amongst other measures.[144]

---

the Black Economic Empowerment Commission. See Business Day TV: The reason BEE trusts are under investigation. https://www.businesslive.co.za/bd/companies/2019-04-24-watch-the-reason-bee-trusts-are-under-investigation/ (last visited 13 June 2019).

142 Basel Committee on Banking Supervision: Global Systemically Important Banks: Assessment Methodology and the Additional Loss Absorbency Requirement. https://www.bis.org/publ/bcbs201.pdf (last visited 13 June 2019).

143 Regular state-owned enterprise issuers include the power utility Eskom and the transport, freight and logistics entity Transnet.

144 Reuters: JSE tightens Rules on Single Stock Futures. https://www.reuters.com/article/jse-futures/jse-tightens-rules-on-single-stock-futures-report-idUSL3628777220090203 (last visited 13 June 2019).

Notes can vary from trade finance instruments such as promissory notes and bills of exchange to exchange traded notes commonly issued by banks.[145]

A participating interest is what an investor receives upon investment in a portfolio of a CIS. These were known as units in previous legislation.[146] The term participating interest covers;

> any interest, undivided share or share whether called a participating interest, unit or by any other name and whether the value of such interest, unit, undivided share or share remains constant or varies from time to time … in a portfolio.[147]

Exchange Traded Funds (ETFs) are listed investment products which track the performance of a group or "basket" of shares, bonds or commodities. These "baskets" are known as indices. An example of a local index is the FTSE/JSE Top 40 Index.[148] ETFs can be bought or sold in the same way as shares.[149] ETFs have been at the centre of the debate regarding the merits or otherwise of active or passive investment in South Africa as in other jurisdictions. Passive ETFs have been punted as preferable to actively managed investments, primarily on the basis of lower costs. A strong view has been expressed by a portfolio manager in South Africa to the effect that actively traded funds outperform passive funds.[150] A contrary view is that

> the general investor should retreat from portfolio management and instead access the market portfolio using low-cost index replication structures via an execution-only approach.[151]

---

145 Exchange Traded Notes JSE. https://www.jse.co.za/trade/equity-market/exchange-traded-products/exchange-traded-notes.

146 Unit Trusts Control Act 54 of 1981.

147 Section 1 CISCA.

148 International indices include FTSE All World Index Series, MSCI World, S&P 100/1200, Russell Global and the global dial.

149 JSE: Exchange Traded Funds. https://www.jse.co.za/trade/equity-market/exchange-traded-products/exchange-traded-funds (last visited 13 June 2019).

150 Johny Lambridis: Why Active Management Beats Passive in South Africa. https://www.prudential.co.za/insights/articlesreleases/why-active-management-beats-passive-in-south-africa/ (last visited 13 June 2019).

151 Desmond Pace: Active Versus Passive Investing: An Empirical Study of the US and European Mutual Funds and ETF's. https://www.emeraldinsight.com/doi/abs/10.1108/S1569-375920160000097006 (last visited 13 June 2019).

The future will tell whether the active has outperformed the passive and vice versa.

Inward listings. In the past foreign entities were not permitted to list on the local stock exchange. However, since 2004 and in order to allow South African investors to obtain foreign exposure through domestic channels, foreign entities have been permitted to list shares on the JSE. This dispensation has been further expanded to include derivative instruments. Equity, debt as well as derivative instruments based on foreign reference assets can be inward listed. South African corporates, trusts, partnerships and private individuals may invest in approved inward listed instruments without restriction.[152] In addition to direct off-shore investments, investments in inward listings act as an effective ZAR (Rand) hedge and are particularly useful in counter-balancing capital pressures in times of ZAR stress.

(b) CISs. These have been touched upon briefly in the discussion of the definition of a security, which includes a participating interest, the normal evidence of interest in the portfolio of a CIS. CISs are a preferred channel for investment in South Africa. Participating interests are to be found regularly in the investment portfolios of individuals and institutions. They carry the advantage of scale in that what one investor, say a retail investor, cannot acquire alone can be acquired by a number of prospective retail investors coming together and pooling their investments. CISs also carry the advantage of professional management. They are generally regarded as safer investments which are made in a highly regulated environment, namely CISCA.

A CIS is defined as a scheme in any form, including an open-ended investment company and by extension, a closed ended investment company[153] whereby members of the public are invited to invest money or assets in a portfolio. The term "mutual fund" is often used interchangeably with CIS.[154] In addition to receiving participating interests for their

152 SARB. Inward Listings. https://www.resbank.co.za/RegulationAndSupervision/FinancialSurveillanceAndExchangeControl/FAQs/Pages/Inward%20listings.aspx (last visited 13 June 2019).

153 An open-end fund is "open" to new investors, and there is no set number of participating interests. Open-end funds always stand ready to buy or sell their participating interests at net asset value whenever an investor chooses to withdraw or deposit money in the fund. Closed-end funds are "closed" to new investors. Like corporate stocks, they are generally issued only once through an initial public offering. See Santoshi Chawla: What is the difference between closed end and open ended funds. https://www.quora.com/What-is-the-difference-between-closed-and-open-ended-funds (last visited 13 June 2019).

154 The most common form of CIS in South Africa is the unit trust. The differences between mutual funds and unit trusts lie in the structure but the end result for the investor is much

investments in CIS portfolios, investors share the risk and benefit of investment in proportion to their participating interest in the CIS portfolio.[155]

A local collective investment scheme is normally established by a CIS manager. The CIS manager is required to be registered in terms of CISCA before it can administer a CIS.[156] An application by the manager or operator of a foreign collective investment scheme to solicit investments in its scheme from members of the South African public may be approved in prescribed circumstances.[157]

The CIS manager is required to appoint either a trustee or a custodian for its CIS, depending on the structure of the scheme.[158] The duties of the trustee or custodian include ensuring that the basis on which the sale, issue, repurchase or cancellation of participatory interests on behalf of the scheme is carried out, is in accordance with CISCA[159] and the relevant deed. A manager is required to publish on a daily basis, the prices of the most expensive class of participating interests which it offers for investment to members of the public. This must include the latest total expense ratio (TER) which is applicable to that portfolio. Publication is required to be on the manager's website and in at least one national newspaper.[160] In addition, the custodian or trustee is required to ensure that the selling or repurchase price of participatory interests is calculated in accordance with CISCA and the relevant deed. The custodian or trustee is also required to enquire into and prepare a report on the administration of the CIS by the CIS manager for each annual accounting period and to

---

the same. On a simple level, a unit trust is established as a trust, while a mutual fund has the structure of a limited liability company. See "Profiles unit trusts and collective investment March 2018." Open ended investment companies and closed ended investment companies would be considered mutual funds.

155 Section 1 CISCA.

156 Section 42 CISCA. Amongst other requirements, the Registrar of Collective Investments is to be satisfied that the deed which the applicant proposes to prepare for the purposes of the collective investment scheme does not contain anything inconsistent with CISCA. The matters which are required to be provided for in deeds for collective investment schemes in securities and property are set out in schedules 1 and 2 of CISCA.

157 Section 65 CISCA. Restrictions on foreign collective investment scheme to carry on business in South Africa.

158 Section 68 CISCA.

159 For instance, a manager may not sell any participating interest at a price which exceeds or is less than the net asset value of that participating interest. Section 94 CISCA.

160 Section 12 of Board Notice 92 of 8 August 2014: Advertising, Marketing and Information Disclosure Requirements For Collective Investment Schemes (Government Gazette 37885).

ensure that there is a legal separation of assets held under custody and that the legal entitlement of investors to such assets is assured.[161]

The deed is the foundational document which remains central to the most common type of CIS (unit trust). Every deed is required to set out the requirements for the administration of a portfolio. Each deed must contain, among other requirements, provisions regulating the matters set out in Schedule 1 of CISCA in respect of CISs in securities and those matters detailed in Schedule 2 in respect of a CISIP.[162] A sample or model master deed to be entered into between the manager of a CIS and the trustee is available on the FSCA website[163] and can be customised for individual schemes.

Those CISs which are structured as corporate vehicles have to comply with the requisite sections of the Companies Act 71 of 2008. In addition, the custodian or trustee, as the case may be, is required to ensure that appropriate internal control systems are maintained and that the records clearly identify the nature and value of all assets under custody, the ownership of each asset and the place where documents of title pertaining to each asset are kept.[164]

The manager is also required to appoint an auditor for the purposes of auditing "the whole of the business of the collective investment scheme administered by it."[165]

The securities, classes of securities, assets or classes of assets which may be included in a portfolio of a CIS in securities are determined in accordance with the relevant board notice.[166]

---

161 Section 70 CISCA.

162 Section 97 CISCA.

163 Model Deed. https://www.fsca.co.za/Regulated%20Entities/Regulated%20Entities%20Documents/CISCA%20-%20Model%20Deed%20for%20CIS%20in%20Property.pdf (last visited 13 June 2019).

164 Section 70 CISCA.

165 Section 73 CISCA. The CIS manager is required to maintain accounting records and prepare annual financial statements in accordance with "generally accepted accounting practice". The auditor must examine the records and statements, "satisfy himself that the accounting records comply with CISCA and that the financial statements are properly drawn up so as to fairly represent the financial position, and the results of the operations of the manager and every portfolio in its collective investment scheme are in accordance with generally accepted accounting practice in the manner required" by CISCA. See section 74 of CISCA. In addition, the auditor has a duty to disclose any irregularity or undesirable practices by the manager "which comes to his or her notice in the ordinary course of fulfilling his or her audit responsibilities or performing other functions in terms" of CISCA. See section 75 of CISCA.

166 BN 90 of 8 August 2014 (Government Gazette No. 37895).

The manner in which securities or assets may be included in a portfolio, as well as the limits (including asset spreads) and conditions in terms of which such securities or assets may be included in a portfolio are set out in the same board notice. The requirements, determination and limits of assets which may be included in a portfolio of a CISIP are set out in a separate notice.[167] The rules for the administration of CISs in participation bonds are also spelt out separately.[168]

As with other aspects of securities regulation and for best practice purposes, regulation of CISs in South Africa is benchmarked against the relevant IOSCO Principles.[169] The March 2015 FSAP carried out by the IMF assessed South Africa's legal and regulatory framework very closely against the relevant IOSCO principles.[170] A number of pertinent observations and recommendations were made by the IMF team.[171] In the normal course of events, the authorities in South Africa would be expected to take note of these observations and recommendations with the aim of addressing the shortcomings identified as necessary.

167 GN 572 of 16 May 2008.

168 BN 65 of 20 June 2014 (Government Gazette No. 37740).

169 IOSCO Principle 24: The regulatory system should set standards for the eligibility, governance, organisation and operational conduct of those who wish to market operate a CIS. IOSCO Principle 25: The regulatory system should provide for rules governing legal form and structure of CISs and segregation and protection of client assets. IOSCO Principle 26: Regulation should require disclosure, as set forth under the principles for issuers, which is necessary to evaluate the suitability of a CIS for a particular investor and the value of the investor's interest in the scheme. Principle 27: Regulation should ensure that there is a proper disclosed basis for asset valuation and the pricing and the redemption of units in a CIS.

170 IMF: South Africa Financial Sector Assessment Program Detailed Assessment of Implementation on the IOSCO Objectives and Principles of Securities Regulation. https://www.imf.org/external/pubs/ft/scr/2015/cr1557.pdf (last visited 13 June 2019).

171 Select observations and recommendations: With respect to IOSCO Principle 24 the IMF stated "... There is a need to significantly enhance the requirements to prohibit, restrict or manage conflict of interest as required by Key Question 12 of the IOSCO Assessment Methodology." With respect to IOSCO Principle 26, the IMF stated: "significant gaps in relation to compliance with the requirements of Principle 26 relates to the lack of a requirement to prepare a legally mandated offering document, to prepare accounts in accordance with high quality, internationally acceptable accounting standards, to use standard formats for initial and periodic disclosures to investors, and to address inaccurate, false or misleading statements ..." With respect to IOSCO Principle 27, the IMF observed: "the regulatory requirements for the evaluation of the CIS securities are very general and there are no requirements on the accounting standards to be used to calculate the NAV of a CIS ... There is a need to significantly enhance the regulatory requirements on the valuation of a CIS's assets and determine the high quality accounting standards used in such valuations ..."

Subsequent FSAPs will always report on whether recommendations in previous FSAPs were taken on board.

One of the tools utilised extensively by the policy and regulatory authorities in South Africa is consultation and close collaboration with respective industry bodies. In the context of CIS, insurance, pensions and other investment interests, the Association for Savings and Investment in South Africa (ASISA) plays a critical role. ASISA "is a registered association of persons carrying on the business (inter alia) of a CIS."[172]

One of the more important functions of ASISA is the classification of South African regulated collective investment scheme portfolios. The classification provides a framework within which portfolios with comparable investment objectives and investment universes are grouped together. It is a key tool for investors and their advisers as it is intended to provide useful information during the consideration of investment choices. The objectives of the ASISA classification standard are to promote investor awareness and understanding of CIS portfolio types, assist with the comparison of CIS portfolios within and across classification categories and assist with the assessment of potential risks of investing in a particular type of CIS portfolio.[173]

(c) Intermediaries: There are numerous intermediaries operating in the financial services industry in South Africa. As with other aspects of securities regulation, the regulation of intermediaries takes cognizance of IOSCO's "Principles for Market Intermediaries". These principles provide for minimum entry standards for market intermediaries, initial and ongoing capital and other prudential requirements. The IOSCO principles further set out the requirement to establish an internal function to deliver compliance standards with respect to internal organisation and operational conduct. The aim is to protect the interests of clients and their assets. There is also a requirement to ensure proper management of risk, and procedures for dealing with the failure of a market intermediary so as to minimise damage and loss to investors. There is also

172 Section 25 CISCA. ASISA was formed in 2008 by members of the Association of Collective Investments (ACI), the Investment Management Association of South Africa (IMASA), the Linked Investment Service Providers Association (LISPA) and the Life Offices' Association (LOA). These associations disbanded, and their staff, assets and activities were transferred to ASISA. ASISA operates as a non-profit company and is empowered by a mandate from the inclusive investment industry to represent it in dealings and consultations with Government and regulators including FSCA. https://www.asisa.org.za/ (last visited 13 June 2019).

173 Martin Hesse: How Collective Investment Schemes are Classified. https://www.iol.co.za/personal-finance/how-collective-investments-are-classified-10406565 (last visited 13 June 2019).

a requirement for processes to reduce the prospect of systemic risk in the event of failure of intermediaries.[174]

The term "intermediary" includes the definition of an "authorised user" in the FMA.[175] Securities services which may be rendered by an authorised user include:

i. the buying or selling of securities for own account or on behalf of another person as a business or incidental to conducting business;
ii. using the trading system or infrastructure of an exchange to buy or sell listed securities;
iii. providing (trading and investment) advice to any person;
iv. the custody and administration of securities;
v. the management of securities and funds;
vi. clearing services; or
vii. settlement services.[176]

In practice therefore, the authorised user can receive and transmit orders where the mandate is execution only or discretionary. The authorised user can also carry out proprietary trading or dealing on its own account, provide advice regarding the value of securities or the advisability of investing in, purchasing, or selling securities. The authorised user can also undertake securities underwriting and the placement of financial instruments.[177]

An exchange is required to provide equitable criteria for the purposes of authorisation, and indeed exclusion, of authorised users. In particular, no person can be admitted as an authorised user unless that person:

> is of good character and high business integrity or in the case of a corporate body, is managed by persons who are of good character and high business integrity" and "complies, or, in the case of a corporate body, is managed by persons or employed persons who comply with the standards of training, experience and other qualifications required by the exchange rules.[178]

174 IOSCO Principles 29–32.

175 Section 1 FMA. "Authorised user" means a person authorised by a licensed exchange to perform one or more securities services in terms of the exchange rules and includes an external authorised user where appropriate. Those intermediaries that are not authorised in terms of the FMA are required to be authorised in terms of other sectoral legislation including the Financial Advisory and Intermediary Services Act 37 of 2002, discussed infra.

176 Section 1 FMA. Clearing and settlement services are addressed separately in this work.

177 Methodology for Assessing Compliance with IOSCO Principles https://www.iosco.org/library/pubdocs/pdf/IOSCOPD562.pdf page 192. (last visited 13 June 2019).

178 Section 17(2) (a) FMA.

In addition, the exchange must impose requirements for the capital adequacy and guarantee and risk management requirements with which authorised users are to comply. The capital adequacy guarantee and risk management requirements have to be prudent although the different categories of authorised users or the different activities of the businesses of authorised users may be taken into account.[179]

The FMA contains additional provisions with respect to the restriction on borrowing against and the pledging of securities belonging to other persons,[180] the recording of details of securities,[181] restrictions on the alienation of securities,[182] segregation of funds[183] and segregation of securities.[184]

The Registrar of the Securities Services is authorised to prescribe a code of conduct for authorised users as well as other participants in the securities services industry.[185] A code of conduct is binding on authorised users, their officers, employees and clients.[186]

At this juncture, authorised users are bound by a code of conduct which survived the repeal of the SSA by the FMA.[187] The code of conduct is in line with section 75 of the FMA (principles of code of conduct) and is largely consistent with the thrust of MifID 2.[188] In terms of this code of conduct, authorised users must:

(i) at all times render securities services honestly, fairly, with due skill, care and diligence in the interests of clients and the integrity of the securities services industry;
(ii) exercise independent professional judgement;
(iii) conduct him or herself in a manner which furthers the objects of the FMA;
(iv) maintain a knowledge of and comply with all applicable laws rules and regulations governing his or her activities.[189]

179 Section 17 (2) (c) FMA.
180 Section 18 FMA.
181 Section 19 FMA.
182 Section 20 FMA.
183 Section 21 FMA.
184 Section 22 FMA.
185 Section 74 (1) FMA Code of Conduct for Regulated Persons.
186 Section 74 (2) FMA Code of Conduct for Regulated Persons.
187 Code of Conduct for Authorised Users, 2005, BN 20 In Government Gazette 27231 of 31 January 2005.
188 Section 75 FMA has additional requirements to uphold the integrity of financial markets and avoidance of fraudulent and misleading advertising, canvassing and marketing.
189 Section 2 of the Code of Conduct. General duties of authorised users.

Other aspects of the code of conduct include:

(i) furnishing of advice (steps to take before giving advice including assessment of the client's circumstances, needs and objectives);[190]

(ii) disclosure to clients (need for factual correctness, plain language, timeous delivery, use of specific monetary terms when referring to all amounts, sums, values, charges, fees and remuneration);[191]

(iii) record keeping (maintenance of proper, complete, accurate and secure records);[192]

(iv) inducements (prohibition of inducements which are likely conflict with any duty the authorised user owes to its clients in respect of securities services provided to those clients);[193]

(v) advertisements (requirement for accurate, complete and unambiguous information about a security or security service, risk of loss and uncertainty of future results must be emphasised and there must be discernment of fact from opinion);[194]

(vi) safekeeping and separation of funds and assets (There must be separation and identification of the assets of the client and the assets of the authorised user. There must also be proper accounting for the assets of each client. Importantly, an authorised user may not utilise the assets of clients to finance business activities.);[195]

(vii) client statements (must be provided at regular intervals). The statements provided to a client must contain enough information to enable the client to produce a set of financial statements, determine the composition of the securities and portfolio held by the authorised user for which the authorised user is accountable to the client and determine the market value of the securities comprising the portfolio;[196]

(viii) internal control and risk management (requirement to employ the resources, procedures and technological systems which are necessary for the effective conduct of business);[197]

(ix) guarantees and insurance cover (to the extent required by the exchange, the authorised user is required to maintain appropriate

190 Section 3 Code of Conduct.
191 Section 4 Code of Conduct.
192 Section 5 Code of Conduct.
193 Section 6 Code of Conduct.
194 Section 7 Code of Conduct.
195 Section 8 Code of Conduct.
196 Section 9 Code of Conduct.
197 Section 10 Code of Conduct.

guarantees for professional indemnity or fidelity insurance cover to mitigate risks inherent in his or her business to which clients may be exposed);[198]

(x) waiver of rights (an authorised user may not request or induce a client to waive any right or benefit conferred on it by the code of conduct).[199]

The most visible authorised user in the securities and capital market environment is the stock broker. A stockbroker is required to be a member of the South African Institute of Stockbrokers[200] and may use the designation "stockbroker", "stockbroker (South Africa)" or "stockbroker (SA)". The South African Institute of Stockbrokers has strict requirements for entry into the stockbroker's learning programme. A candidate has to complete a set syllabus and pass the exams prior to admission as a stockbroker. After qualification the stockbroker is required to comply with continuing professional development obligations. In addition, a stockbroker is bound by a code of conduct which is in line with the FMA and addresses such areas as the integrity of financial markets, independence and objectivity, conflict of interest, obligations towards clients (including fairness and the provision of adequate information to clients), confidentiality and the manner of dealing with irregularities and complaints.[201]

The FMA applies to authorised users as defined. This means "person(s) authorised by a licensed exchange to perform one or more securities services in terms of exchange rules ..." In other words, the FMA has limited application. Other financial services providers carrying out securities services not covered by the FMA would otherwise fall outside the regulatory net. This gap is covered by the Financial Advisory and Intermediary Services Act (FAIS).[202] FAIS applies to "financial services providers" who furnish advice or render an "intermediary service".[203] In terms of FAIS, an intermediary service other than the furnishing of advice includes any act by any person which results in a

> client ... entering into any transaction in respect of a financial product with a product supplier or buying, selling or otherwise dealing in, ...

198 Section 11 Code of Conduct.

199 Section 12 Code of Conduct.

200 Section 1 FMA.

201 South African Institute of Stockbrokers. https://www.sais.co.za/ (last visited 13 June 2019).

202 Act 37 of 2002 supra.

203 Section 1 FAIS.

> managing, administering, keeping safe custody, maintaining or servicing a financial product purchased by a client from a product supplier or in which the client has invested …[204]

In order to avoid confusion, FAIS specifically states that it does not apply to the "rendering of financial services by any authorised user …"[205]

FAIS recognises the following categories of financial services provider which are relevant to securities:[206]

i. Category II (discretionary FSPs);
ii. Category IIA (hedge fund FSPs);
iii. Category III (administrative FSPs); and
iv. Category I (FSPs who do not belong to any of the foregoing categories of FSP).

A Category II FSP is one "that renders intermediary services of a discretionary nature as regards the choice of a particular financial product from a range of financial products including shares in companies and instruments such as debentures, securitised debt, money market instruments (and instruments which entitle an investor to subscribe to, acquire, dispose of or convert any of the foregoing instruments) and participating interests in CISs".[207] A CIS manager falls within the definition of a Category II FSP.

A Category IIA (hedge fund) FSP

> renders intermediary services of a discretionary nature in relation to a particular hedge fund or funds of hedge funds.

204 Section 1 FAIS. This definition extends to CIS managers, fund and asset managers, as well as administrators. CIS managers are discussed infra.

205 Section 45 FAIS. Other financial services providers specifically excluded from the application of FAIS include clearing members, clearinghouses, central securities depositories, licensed exchanges and participants authorised in terms of the FMA.

206 Categories of FSPs, Section 3 of BN 194 of 15 December 2017: Determination of Fit and Proper Requirements (Government Gazette 41321).

207 Section 2 of BN 79 of 8 August 2003: Codes of Conduct for Administrative and Discretionary FSPs as read with Section 1 FAIS. The definition of "financial product" covers a number of other financial products which are beyond the scope of this study, including long or short-term insurance contracts policies referred to in the Long Term Insurance Act, 1998 (Act 52 of 1998) and the Short-Term Insurance Act (Act 53 of 1998) and benefits provided by pension fund organisations (as defined in section 1 (1) of the Pension Funds Act 24 of 1956) and friendly societies (referred to in the Friendly Societies Act 25 of 1956).

The services are required to be in connection with a particular financial product from a similar range of financial products to that which may be advised on by a Category II FSP.[208]

A Category III FSP is one "that renders intermediary services" in respect of similar financial products to those on which a Category II FSP provides advice except that the Category III FSP acts on the "instructions of the client or another FSP and through the method of bulking ."[209]

A Category I is a catch-all provision which covers FSPs which are not otherwise included in Categories II, IIA and III of FSP.[210]

Whereas, authorised users to which the FMA refers are required to demonstrate certain technical competencies and experience as set out in that Act,[211] FSPs to which FAIS applies are required to comply with the competence requirements set out in chapter 3 of the "Determination of Fit and Proper Requirements".[212] Subject to exemptions in certain cases, specific requirements are set out for FSPs with respect to minimum experience, minimum qualifications and regulatory examinations.[213]

The impact of the conduct as well as the misconduct of the originators, providers, distributors and investors in over-the-counter derivatives has received wide coverage. Relatively speaking, South Africa has a sizeable over-the-counter derivatives industry. In the wake and aftermath of the GFC, the NT as the policy maker in South Africa, together with the financial sectoral regulators, took note of the lessons from the crisis which emanated from the abuse of over-the-counter derivatives products.

---

208 Section 3 (c) BN 194 of 15 December 2017: Determination of Fit and Proper Requirements (Government Gazette 41321) as read with section 2 (1) Chapter II, Part 1 (definition of "hedge fund FSP") and section 2 (1) (a) Chapter I, Part 1 (definition of "administrative FSP") BN 79 supra.

209 BN 79 supra as read with Section 1 (1) FAIS. Around 2005, a scandal broke out within South African pension fund industry regarding the secret profits earned by pension fund administrators from the bulking of pension funds. Because the profits withheld from the pension funds were not available to the funds when they were earned, they were not applied in generating returns earned by other assets managed in the funds. See Gareth Stokes: "It takes years to undo a financial scandal". https://www.fanews.co.za/article/life-insurance/9/general/1202/it-takes-years-to-undo-a-financial-scandal/104. (last visited 13 June 2019). Category III FSPs are often referred to as administrative FSPs.

210 Section 3 BN 194 supra.

211 Footnotes 178 and 179 supra.

212 BN 194 supra.

213 The Determination of Fit and Proper Requirements for Financial Services Providers (Board Notice 106 of 2008) has introduced the financial services industry to a new concept – "regulatory examinations". Stephanie McKenzie: Regulatory Examinations, an overview. http://financialmarketsjournal.co.za/oldsite/13thedition/printedarticles/regulatoryexams.htm (last visited 13 June 2019).

Consequently, the NT, with an eye to reform, commissioned a study by PricewaterhouseCoopers which it utilised as the base for its report entitled "Regulating Over-the-Counter Derivatives Markets in South Africa".[214] Amongst other contextual observations, the report estimated that the outstanding notional amounts as at June 2012 for OTC derivatives was valued at R27.7 trillion. This amount includes interbank trades between domestic and foreign banks, between domestic banks, and other non-financial participants including corporates. The most common type of derivative asset class, accounting for over 85 per cent of transactions traded in the domestic market, was identified as the interest rate derivative at an estimated outstanding notional amount of R24.3 trillion.

The need was felt to specifically acknowledge the existence of financial services providers offering services in the field of over-the-counter derivatives in addition to related regulatory reform developments.[215] Consequently, an intermediary designated "OTC derivative provider" (ODP) has been recognised. An ODP is defined as a person (or entity) who as a regular feature of its business, transacts as principal, originates, issues or sells OTC derivatives or makes a market in OTC derivatives.[216] On 27 July 2018, the FSCA issued Code Standard 1 of 2018 "Criteria for Authorisation of ODPs"[217] which emphasises capital adequacy, fit and proper requirements, honesty and integrity, competency, operational ability, financial soundness, risk management and internal control, compliance function, business continuity planning and record-keeping and data retention.

Other variations on the function of "broker" including dealers, broker dealers and prime dealers are all covered by the definition of authorised user in the FMA or financial services provider in FAIS. Aspects of the activities of prime brokerages which offer services including credit facilities to clients such as hedge funds, may not be adequately regulated at this point in time. The provision of credit by a prime brokerage falls squarely within the purview of "shadow banking" or "non-bank financial intermediation" as it is to be known in the future. The regulation of this

---

214 NT: Regulating Over-The-Counter Derivatives Markets in South Africa. http://www.treasury.gov.za/otc/Regulating%20over-the-counter%20(OTC)%20derivates%20markets%20in%20South%20Africa.pdf (last visited 13 June 2019). Getting current information on the sector of financial services is difficult because transactions are not carried out in a public marketplace and trade repositories to be discussed infra, are only just becoming operational.

215 Central counterparties and trade repositories infra.

216 Section 1 Schedule to FMA Regulations (GNR 98 of 9 February 2018) (Government Gazette 41433).

217 FSCA: https://www.fsca.co.za/Notices/Conduct%20Standard%201%20of%202018%20-%20%20Criteria%20for%20Authorisation%20of%20ODPs.pdf (last visited 13 June 2019).

activity is still causing challenges for regulators in a significant number of jurisdictions.[218] Shadow banking is often thought to comprise private credit intermediation occurring outside the formal banking system. As an example, the National Credit Act[219] (NCA) is regarded as a response to the unmet needs and preferences of willing borrowers and lenders. It extends necessary protections particularly to the borrower. Shadow banking is therefore considered as enabling borrowers or issuers to access new outlets for capital raising when bank lending is unavailable.[220]

Shadow banking, as stated, is regarded as the provision and receiving of credit facilities outside of the formal banking system. It would appear that the provision of credit by prime brokerage houses is not covered by legislation that is alternative to the Banking Act 94 of 1990. Note that the NCA is intended, amongst other outcomes to

> promote a fair and non-discriminatory marketplace for access to consumer credit and for that purpose to provide for the general regulation of consumer credit and improved standards of consumer protection ...

Clearly the emphasis of the NCA is on retail consumer credit and retail consumer protection and is not designed to cover "self-sufficient" financial engineers such as hedge funds accessing credit from nonbanking financial entities.

(d) Trading platforms. These are the fulcrum for the majority of investment activity in advanced economies and increasingly, in emerging economies. Trading platforms provide a marketplace, whether public or private, for the purchase and sale of securities.

The most common type of trading platform is the traditional stock exchange examples of which include the New York Stock Exchange, the London stock exchange, the Australian Stock Exchange and the JSE, just to name a few.

---

218 On 25 June 2018, the Financial Stability Board stated: "With regard to the work to transform shadow banking into resilient market-based finance, the FSB has decided to replace the term "shadow banking" with the term "non-bank financial intermediation" in future communications. The new terminology emphasises the forward-looking aspects of the FSB's work to enhance the resilience of non-bank financial intermediation. See FSB Reviews financial Vulnerabilities and Deliverables for G20 Summit. http://www.fsb.org/2018/10/fsb-reviews-financial-vulnerabilities-and-deliverables-for-g20-summit/ (last visited 13 June 2019).

219 Act 34 of 2005.

220 IMF Shadow Banking and Market Based Finance Tobias Adrian, International Monetary Fund Helsinki September 14, 2017. https://www.imf.org/en/News/Articles/2017/09/13/sp091417-shadow-banking-and-market-based-finance (last visited 13 June 2019).

Most of the major stock exchanges have transformed from mutualised to demutualised entities. A number are public companies listed on themselves, such as the JSE or listed on a competing exchange such as the Bombay Stock Exchange (BSE) which is listed on the rival National Stock Exchange. The BSE is India's largest, Asia's oldest and the world's 10th largest stock exchange by market capitalisation.[221]

Awareness of the utility of stock exchanges as vehicles for accessing or mobilising funding for capital and strategic investments has grown tremendously since the establishment of the Antwerp Stock Exchange reputedly as the first stock exchange in 1460. In spite of this, the Amsterdam Stock Exchange is considered the oldest in the world although it was established in 1602 by the Dutch East India Company (Verenigde Oostindische Compagnie or VOC) which also issued the first shares on that exchange.[222]

Today, membership of the World Federation of Exchanges (WFE) numbers 67 members with solid representation from 21 emerging economies.[223] Tunisia and Nairobi are the WFE's newest members.[224] One should be aware of other stock exchanges operating in Sub- Saharan Africa.[225]

---

221 Amit Mudgill: BSE creates history! Exchange lists at Rs 1,085, 34.62per cent premium over issue price. https://economictimes.indiatimes.com/markets/stocks/news/bse-creates-history-exchange-lists-at-rs-1085-34-62-premium-over-issue-price/articleshow/56947266.cms. (last visited 13 June 2019).

222 Amit Lolwai: Which Is the Oldest Stock Exchange in the World. https://timesofindia.indiatimes.com/Which-is-the-oldest-stock-exchange-in-the-world/articleshow/1491593.cms? (last visited 13 June 2019).

223 These exchanges are the Abu Dhabi Securities Exchange, the Amman Stock Exchange, Bolsa de Comercio de Buenos Aires, Bolsa de Comercio de Santiago, Bolsa de Valores de Colombia, Bolsa de Valores de Lima, Bolsa Mexicana de Valores, Borsa Istanbul, Bourse de Casablanca, BSE India Limited, Bursa Malaysia, Dhaka Stock Exchange Limited, Dubai Financial Market, the Egyptian Stock Exchange, Indonesia Stock Exchange, Johannesburg Stock Exchange, Muscat Securities Market, Nairobi Securities Exchange, National Stock Exchange of India Limited, Nigerian Stock Exchange, Philippine Stock Exchange, Qatar Stock Exchange, Saudi Stock Exchange, Shanghai Stock Exchange, Shenzhen Stock Exchange, Stock Exchange of Mauritius, Stock Exchange of Thailand, Taipei Exchange and the Taiwan Stock Exchange. See WFE Members. https://www.world-exchanges.org/membership-events (last visited 13 June 2019).

224 Tunis Stock Exchange, a new member of the World Federation of Exchanges. See African Markets. https://www.african-markets.com/en/stock-markets/bvmt/tunis-stock-exchange-a-new-member-of-the-world-federation-of-exchanges (last visited 13 June 2019).

225 These exchanges include the Botswana Stock Exchange, Malawi Stock Exchange, Maputo Stock Exchange, Dar Es Salaam Stock Exchange, Ghana Stock Exchange the Uganda stock exchange, Lusaka Stock Exchange and the Zimbabwe Stock Exchange. See Economy Watch: Stock Markets in Sub-Saharan Africa: http://www.economywatch.com/stock-markets-in-world/sub-saharan-africa.html (last visited 13 June 2019). There is also the Bourse Régionale des Valeurs Mobilières which is the regional stock exchange for the West African Economic and Monetary Union (WAEMU) based in Côte d'Ivoire and

Asia has a fair representation of exchanges.[226] Latin America and the Caribbean also have a significant number of stock exchanges.[227] The remaining stock exchanges in the European region are not enumerated herein as the region is generally well represented by membership on the WFE.

The purpose of the foregoing elaborate identification of stock exchanges in various regions and jurisdictions around the world is to demonstrate the practically universal embrace of the stock exchange as a critical platform for raising capital for the purposes of bolstering economic activity.

Over the last 10 years, the landscape for trading platforms has changed considerably. Emerging jurisdictions like South Africa have taken a keen interest in developments in Europe. The Markets in Financial Instruments Directive (MiFID), 2004/39/EC, (MiFID I) which took effect on November 1, 2007 has been of particular interest, purporting as it did to update the "old Investment Services Directive." MiFID I represented a significant reform of financial services regulation in the European Union. MiFID I sets out a comprehensive regulatory regime covering investment services and financial markets in the European Union. One of the aims of MiFID I was to do away with barriers to cross-border trading and to recognise competition into the European investment services industry. Importantly, MiFID I sought to remove the concentration rule. In other words, Member States of the EU could no longer require investment firms to route orders only to stock exchanges. This meant that exchanges would in future face competition from multilateral trading facilities (MTFs) which, amongst other platforms included non-exchange trading

---

serving 7 other countries namely Benin, Burkina Faso, Guinea-Bissau, Mali, Niger, Senegal and Togo.

226 These exchanges include Baku Stock Exchange is Kazakhstan Stock Exchange, Kyrgyz Stock Exchange, Mongolian Stock Exchange, Nepal Stock, Islamabad Stock Exchange, Karachi Stock Exchange, Lahore Stock Exchange, Colombo Stock Exchange and Tashkent Republican Stock Exchange Stock Exchanges in Asia. See WFE Members and Affiliates. https://www.world-exchanges.org/membership-events (last visited 13 June 2019).

227 These exchanges include the Buenos Aires Stock Exchange, Bahamas International Stock Exchange, Barbados Stock Exchange, Bolsa Boliviana de Valores, Brazilian Mercantile and Exchange, Costa Rica Stock Exchange, Bolsa de Valores de la Republica Dominicana, Bolsa de Valores de Quito, Bolsa de Valores de El Salvador, Bolsa de Valores Nacional (Guatemala), Bolsa Centroamericana de Valores (Honduras), Jamaican Stock Exchange, Bolsa de Valores de Nicaragua, Bolsa de Valores de Panama, Portafolio de Valores (Paraguay), Bolsa de Valores de Lima, Trinidad and Tobago Stock Exchange, Bolsa de Valores de Montevideo and Bolsa de Valores de Caracas. See List of Stock Exchanges in Latin America and the Caribbean. https://stocknewser.blogspot.com/2012/03/list-of-stock-exchanges-in-latin.html (last visited 13 June 2019).

platforms and systematic internalizers.[228] These platforms are normally operated by entities such as banks and investment firms which systematically execute client orders internally on their own account rather than sending them to exchanges. In order to ensure a level playing field with exchanges, MTFS were to be subjected to similar pre- and post-trade transparency requirements as the exchanges in addition to providing full information on trading activity to the market.

MiFID I also sought to entrench the "best execution" rule which meant that when firms executed client orders, they had to take all reasonable steps to deliver the best possible result for their clients. This meant that investment firms had to take a variety of factors into account including the price of the financial instrument, speed of execution of the order and cost.[229]

The focus on best execution is because of the information asymmetry arising between the service provider and the client. In the normal course of events, investors and prospective investors do not really have the wherewithal to determine whether the broker or investment firm that executed orders on their behalf actually acted in their best interests. This is owing to them probably not being able to access the necessary information that would enable them to assess the quality of the service. But even if such information were freely available, in reality, investors would in all likelihood not have the time or appropriate knowledge to assess detailed disclosures related to the execution of their orders. Neither would they have the means to make an effective comparative evaluation of the execution policy of the broker.[230]

The G20, an international forum of governments and central banks drawn from a number of advanced and developing countries including South Africa, was also active in the area of financial markets reform. In 2010, at a summit held in Seoul, South Korea, the G20 launched an action plan "with the purpose of achieving strong, sustainable and balanced

228 Other platforms which have emerged include dark pools.

229 To illustrate, if venue A offered an instrument for 100 euros and the costs of executing on that venue (e.g. exchange fees, settlement fees, etc.) amounted to 5 euros (making the total consideration equal to 105 euros), while another venue B offered the same instrument for 102 euros with costs of execution equal to 2 euros, the investment firm was compelled to execute the client order to buy on venue B. This was in view of the fact that the total consideration of 104 euros delivered a better result for the client. In essence, best execution is a core principle of MiFID and is essential for investor protection.

230 James Hamilton: Markets in Financial Instruments Directive (MiFID): Broad Reforms to EU Financial Services Regulation. http://business.cch.com/securitiesLaw/news/MiFID%20whitepaper.pdf (last visited 13 June 2019).

growth".[231] In this commitment, the G20 called for significant policy actions including reform of the financial sector. The G20 also

> … called on IOSCO to develop by June 2011 and report to the Financial Stability Board recommendations to promote markets' integrity and efficiency to mitigate the risks posed to the financial system by the latest technological developments.[232]

IOSCO noted that the evolution of markets and, in particular, advances in and expansion of the use of technology in trading had had numerous impacts which facilitated the establishment of globally competitive markets. These developments enabled market participants to reduce transaction time to just fractions of a second. IOSCO went on to observe that the advances had provided benefits which included the generation of electronic audit trails, the enhancement of order and trade transparency, and the ability of markets and market participants to develop and apply automated risk controls. The advances also enabled competent authorities to monitor the establishment and use of those risk controls.

IOSCO further cautioned that the various benefits arising from technological advances should not be permitted to overshadow the risks that these innovations pose to the efficiency and integrity of markets; that these changes raised issues that should be addressed by regulators in order to maintain the integrity of financial markets; and that any change to the structure of financial markets should be assessed with respect to the objective of preserving their fundamental role for the economy.

In addition, IOSCO observed that the rapid pace of technological progress and regulatory changes in many jurisdictions had resulted in increased competition, in particular between trading venues; that this has yielded a number of benefits, amongst which are lower trading fees and enhanced potential for innovation as venue operators aim to compete to attract liquidity; that as part of this, however, competition had also led to fragmentation of markets, both in terms of liquidity and information; that this meant that, in many jurisdictions, the search for best price by market participants (including in the context of providing investors with best possible execution) now involved the consideration of multiple sources of

231 The G20 Seoul Summit Declaration, 11–12 November 2010, available at https://www.treasury.gov/resource-center/international/Documents/1%20%20FINAL%20SEOUL%20COMMUNIQUE.pdf (last visited 13 June 2019).

232 Regulatory Issues Raised by the Impact of Technological Changes on Market Integrity and Efficiency Consultation Report. http://www.iosco.org/library/pubdocs/pdf/IOSCOPD354.pdf. Page 6 (last visited 13 June 2019).

liquidity as well as possibly increased search costs; and that these sources of liquidity included exchanges and non-exchange trading venues, such as alternative trading systems (ATSs) in the United States and Canada and MTFs in Europe and brokers' internal crossing networks as well as lit and dark liquidity. As a result, IOSCO noted that equity markets, for which on-exchange trading was prominent, had become more fragmented and less transparent in some instances. In effect, the further development of multiple trading venues resulted in the liquidity of particular shares often being split amongst different pools of liquidity operating with or without pre-trade transparency. As such, IOSCO warned, the full benefits of post trade transparency could be undermined in some countries by the costs and complexity of market data consolidation.[233]

A significant initiative, amongst many others, in the context of trading platforms is IOSCO's publication entitled "SME Financing through Capital Markets"[234] in which the author was the pen holder. This publication explored the environment for financing of small and medium-sized enterprises through the capital markets and existing impediments. The publication went on to make recommendations regarding the improvement of accessibility of capital markets by small and medium-sized enterprises, including the need to deepen capital markets by influencing the attitude of institutional investors, attracting more retail investors through educational programs and financial inclusion, differential listing requirements and appropriate incentives. The report observed that, many jurisdictions had implemented junior boards with the aim of assisting SMEs to access market-based financing, with mixed results.

It was against the background of the foregoing international reform initiatives that policymakers and regulators in South Africa advanced their own financial initiatives.[235] Indeed, the promulgation of the FMA for instance, which effected significant improvements over the SSA, was preceded by an extensive consultation process lasting some 5 to 6 years. The drafting panel included influential incumbents with vested interests,[236] which perhaps explained the option not to push ahead with the full path of reform initiated and implemented by MiFID I particularly in the area of the facilitation of the licensing of MTFs and ATSs which would have

233 Regulatory Issues Raised by the Impact of Technological Changes on Market Integrity and Efficiency Consultation Report. http://www.iosco.org/library/pubdocs/pdf/IOSCOPD354.pdf ibid.

234 SME Financing Through Capital Markets Final Report. https://www.iosco.org/library/pubdocs/pdf/IOSCOPD493.pdf (last visited 13 June 2019).

235 FMA and Financial Sector Regulation Act supra.

236 JSE and Strate (Pty) Limited the only exchange and central securities depository.

resulted in an immediate and impactful effect on competition in trading platforms. Currently, in South Africa, it is not possible to apply for a trading platform license except as a fully-fledged stock exchange. In spite of these artificial and retrogressive measures, some competition has been introduced through the licensing of additional stock exchanges.[237] The reception of new exchanges has not been smooth. There has been a flurry of legal actions against the FSB SA and ZAR X by the incumbent initially alone and subsequently in conjunction with another newcomer, 4AX.[238]

The securities and capital markets area is dynamic. Even as the policymakers and regulators in South Africa go about implementing the regulatory reforms in accordance with their cautious agenda, countries in the European Union are now implementing MiFID II which is described as "a revamped version of MiFID I ... designed to offer greater protection for investors and inject more transparency into all asset classes: from equities to fixed income, exchange traded funds ..."[239]

A ground-breaking MiFID II requirement is that investment research must in future be paid for from a fund manager's own account, which may be recoverable by raising fees, or by way of a ring-fenced client research-payment account. Although EU regulators permit research charges to be collected alongside transaction commissions, subject to strict conditions, there has to be no link to transaction value or volume. This move to an

237 A2X, ZAR-X, Equity Express and 4AX.

238 In the first case, the JSE successfully challenged the FSB SA's decision to issue a conditional license to ZAR X before the Appeal Board. See JSE Limited / The Registrar of Securities Services: ZAR X Exchange Licence – Case Number A8/2016. In another appeal before Appeal Board, the JSE and 4AX failed to have the FSB SA's second decision to license ZAR X set aside. See JSE Limited and 4 Africa Exchange (Pty) LTD and The Registrar of Securities Services and ZAR X (Pty) Limited – Case Number A25/2016. A dogged 4AX has taken the Appeal Board's judgment on review to the High Court. See 4 Africa Exchange (Pty) Limited and The Registrar of Securities Services, ZAR X (Pty) Limited, L.T.C. Harms N.O., Afrifocus Securities (Pty) Limited, Anchor Securities Stockbrokers (Pty) Limited, Saxo Capital Markets South Africa (Pty) limited, Senwes Limited and Senwesbel Limited: Case 17/20474 (High Court of South Africa, South Gauteng). The founding affidavit of the CEO of 4AX makes alarming reading particularly in its presumptuous familiarity as well as its bold, speculative and clearly misleading impunity, inter alia, in its illusory and malignant personal attacks on the regulators including the author with whom she has never held a conversation. Honest and unconflicted regulators can really only look to the courts for protection from the actions of litigants of this curious nature. The question on many commentator's lips is: why the frittering by this newcomer of its limited shareholder contributed seed capital on this relentless and onslaught on a fellow newcomer. Should it not be concentrating its efforts and resources on securing more listings and building its business?

239 Phillip Stafford: What is MiFID II and how will it affect EU's financial industry? https://www.ft.com/content/ae935520-96ff-11e7-b83c-9588e51488a0 (last visited 13 June 2019).

unbundled model, which is yet to be adopted in South Africa, is expected to limit the age-old use of commissions or "soft dollar" arrangements as an indivisible cost of research and is set to disrupt the industry globally.[240]

Stock exchanges in South Africa are regulated in terms of Chapter III of the FMA. A stock exchange is defined as "a person who constitutes, maintains and provides an infrastructure:

(a) for bringing together buyers and sellers of securities;
(b) for matching bids and offers for securities of multiple buyers and sellers; and
(c) whereby a matched bid and offer constitutes a transaction."[241]

Applications for exchange licences are detailed and include prescribed requirements for assets and resources,[242] as well as governance and operational requirements.[243]

---

240 Sarah Jane Mahmud, Alison Williams and Ben Elliott: The future of investment research post-MiFID II. https://www.bloomberg.com/professional/blog/future-investment-research-post-mifid-ii/ (last visited 13 June 2019).

241 A number of initiatives have been introduced into the South African investment landscape, to address apartheid's legacy of unequal distribution of wealth within the country. These initiatives have to an extent been bolstered by BBBEE legislation and practice. One of these initiatives is the use of special-purpose vehicles (SPVs) funded in a number of ways, including vendor finance, finance from future dividends or bank funding serviced by dividends and capital growth to acquire usually minority shareholdings in predominantly listed entities. Shareholders in the SPVs would be investors classified as "previously disadvantaged individuals" whose investment in the SPV was generally locked until the purchase of shares had been paid off. As expected, when the shares were paid off, investors would be anticipated to want to liquidate their investments. A number of formal and informal mechanisms were set up within SPVs to facilitate the matching of buyers and sellers thereby inadvertently falling within the definition of exchange. It therefore became necessary to issue BN 68 of 11 July 2014: Financial Services Board: Directive and Guideline No. 1 of 2014: Directive and Guideline Regarding Infrastructures Provided by Companies Facilitating Trading in Their Own Securities. https://www.greengazette.co.za/notices/financial-markets-act-19-2012-financial-services-board-directive-and-guideline-no-1-of-2014_20140711-GGN-37805-00068.pdf. The SPV structure was also utilised in the case of investments in agricultural and other cooperatives.

242 Specific requirements for assets and resources for exchanges, as well as central securities depositories, clearinghouses and trade repositories were set out in section 8, chapter V "Assets and Resources Requirements for Certain Market Infrastructures", of the FMA Regulations GNR 98 of 9 February 2018.

243 Sections 7 and 8 of the FMA. The requirements include: clear and transparent governance arrangements to promote the safety and efficiency of the exchange; demonstration of the fitness and propriety of members of exchanges controlling body and senior management; arrangements for the efficient and effective surveillance of all transactions effected through the exchange as well as the supervision of authorised users; arrangements for the efficient and effective monitoring of compliance by issuers of securities listed on the exchange with the exchange's listing requirements; arrangements to efficiently and effectively manage material risks associated with the operation of exchange; arrangements

Amongst other conditions, an exchange licence is required to specify the terms and conditions of the licence, the categories of securities that may be listed on the exchange, the registered office of the exchange within South Africa and the places where the exchange may be operated, and a stipulation that the exchange may not be operated at any other place without the prior written consent of the FSCA (previously FSB SA).

The functions of a licence exchange are substantially in line with the requirements for licensing.[244]

There are additional requirements set out in the listings rules with respect to the actual listings and trading ecosystem.[245] These requirements mirror the governance and operational matters considered in the application for a license.[246]

Importantly, the rules of the exchange are required to provide an equitable criteria for authorisation and exclusion of authorised users including a demonstration of good character and high business integrity

---

for efficient and effective security and backup procedures to ensure the integrity of the records of transactions effected with the exchange; insurance, guarantee, compensation fund or other warranty to enable the exchange to provide compensation as required; arrangements for the efficient and effective clearing and settlement of transactions effected through the exchange and for the management of settlement risk; implementation of an effective and reliable infrastructure to facilitate the trading of securities listed on the exchange; and submission of a copy of the proposed exchange rules; and submission of a copy of the proposed listing requirements.

244 Section 10 of the FMA. There may at times appear to be an overlap in the requirements for the licencing of authorised users and the requirements for the listing of an exchange.

245 The JSE, the oldest stock exchange in the country, has listings requirements for different instruments including equity, debt and derivatives. The rules are regularly updated with the intention of remaining abreast of best practice and approved by the regulatory authority as required. All the new stock exchanges have their own listings requirements which have been approved by the regulator.

246 Section 11 of the FMA. Additional coverage in the rule includes the need to show how securities may be listed, removed or suspended from the exchanges list; requirements with which issuers of listed securities are required to comply; the standards of conduct required to be met by issuers of listed securities and their directors, officers and agents; the standards of disclosure and corporate governance that issuers of listed securities are required to meet; certain requirements for the investigation and discipline of issuers or their officers in the event of a contravention of the listing requirements; the imposition of specified penalties on listed entities in the event of failure to comply with the listing requirements including reprimand, a fine not exceeding R7.5 million, disqualification, suspension or termination of listing.

and appropriate standards of training, experience and specified qualifications.[247] Section 17 of the FMA sets out further requirements.[248]

Authorised users are required to comply with specific requirements which impose a restriction on borrowing against and re-pledging of securities belonging to other persons, marking of or recording details of securities, restriction on alienation of securities, segregation of funds and segregation of securities.[249]

There are 371 companies listed on the JSE, of which 325 are listed on the main board, and 46 are listed on the junior board known as Alt X. The new exchanges are in the development phase and are working on building critical mass. For instance, A2X currently has 18 secondary listed companies whose primary listing is on the JSE. As at 30 September 2018, ZAR X and 4AX had 5 and 4 listed companies respectively. Regardless of the listings and other activity on all the exchanges, the regulator will need to adapt to a demanding and challenging multi-exchange environment.

Securities listed on the JSE include equity (e.g. ordinary and preference shares), debt instruments (e.g. bonds and exchange traded notes), derivatives (e.g. put and call options including single stock futures and

247 Section 17 (2) (a) FMA. See also discussion of SAIS requirements, supra.

248 These additional requirements include criteria for authorisation of the security services that authorised users may provide; capital adequacy and risk management requirements for authorised users; the efficient, honest, transparent and fair manner for transactions in listed securities to be affected by authorised users; clearing and settlement of listed securities; determination of transactions to be cleared by the exchange, the circumstances in which the exchange may refuse to clear transaction securities and the monitoring of settlement obligations of authorised users and their clients in the case where the exchange is not appointed a clearinghouse to clear transactions effected through the exchange; circumstances in which a transaction in listed securities may be declared void by the exchange; approval of nominees of an authorised user; circumstances in which trading in any listed security may be suspended or halted; the recording of transactions effected through the exchange, monitoring of compliance by authorised users with exchange rules and directors and surveillance for the purposes of the FMA, the exchange rules and directors; the circumstances and manner in which an authorised user may advertise or canvas for business; complaints handling; steps to be taken for the purposes of investigative and disciplinary functions relating to an authorised user or its employees; disclosure by authorised users to their clients of their fees for services rendered and the method of calculation; circumstances under which an exchange may limit the revocation of any settlement instructions given by an authorised user to its client; the manner in which an authorised user acting as an interdealer broker is required to conduct its interdealer broking services; and the circumstances in which an authorised user may or may not transact in listed securities using the services of an interdealer broker who is not an authorised user.

249 Sections 18 to 22.

warrants) and exchange traded funds.[250] Securities listed on the new exchanges are similar to those offered by the JSE, although, interestingly, A2X which is patterned on Chi-X is required, as a condition of its licence, to secure the approval of the entities listed on the JSE to which it accords a secondary listing. In the author's view, this condition is yet another example of the regulator's retrogressive caution which serves to safeguard the status quo at the expense of competition.[251] Chi-X Australia for instance, which was launched in November 2011, is not required to secure the consent of the companies to which it extends a secondary listing. As the first alternative trading venue to the Australian Securities Exchange (ASX), Chi-X Australia began with as little as 8 tradeable stocks and is now offering the full suite of 2,100 ASX-listed companies.[252] The Chi X model is also to be found in Europe, Asia and Canada.

In terms of the FMA, the term "securities" means listed and unlisted securities, including shares, depositary receipts and other equities in public companies and derivative instruments.

Although the FMA accorded the Minister of Finance the power to prescribe requirements for the regulation of unlisted securities,[253] the position has remained precarious for investors in such instruments in the absence of a framework with similar protections to those provided for investors in listed securities. The jurisdiction of the securities regulator as a consequence is still restricted to listed securities. This lacuna has caused well documented hardship for investors which were lured into investing in certain unlisted securities.[254] Although companies with

250 As the debate around active versus passive investment has picked up momentum, ETFs including the well-known Satrix have gained in popularity. Satrix, which is structured as a type of CIS is designed to enable investors to buy shares in the largest 40 JSE-listed companies. Satrix was started in 2000 with the launch of the Satrix 40 Exchange-Traded Fund (ETF) as the first ETF to be launched in South Africa. See Brett Landman, CEO of the Satrix Exchange-Traded Fund: What is Satrix 40. https://www.fin24.com/money/money-clinic/what-is-satrix-40-20111110 (last visited 13 June 2019).

251 The 2018 Financial Markets Review supra at page 111 notes: "Apart from certain regulatory requirements relating to dark pools, there is no regulatory framework for alternative trading venues in South Africa. The FMRC recommends that regulators consider developing such a regulatory regime to ensure level playing fields."

252 Genevieve Wood: What is Chi-X and how does it work? http://blog.openmarkets.com.au/what-is-chi-x-and-how-does-it-work (last visited 13 June 2019).

253 Section 5 FMA.

254 For instance, the Registrar of Securities Services within the FSB SA (now FSCA), could not intervene in cases where schemes which turned out to be scams, had been structured around the creation of a number of companies and the issue of shares to investors in those entities which remained unlisted. One such saga involved the company Sharemax.

unlisted shares fell under the jurisdiction of the Registrar of Companies, which functionary did not have jurisdiction to enforce investor protection provisions similar to those provided under the FMA.

The Minister has recently issued regulations ("FMA Regulations"),[255] but did not extend the FMA regulatory framework to unlisted shares.[256] The lacuna has possibly been addressed indirectly and to a limited extent by the application and implementation of the FSRA[257] which defines a "financial service" to include the "offering, promoting, marketing or distributing" of a financial instrument.[258] The definition of a financial instrument includes a share as defined in the Companies Act.[259]

In terms of the FSRA a person may not provide a financial service unless the person does so in accordance with "a licence in terms of a specific financial sector law …"[260] A contravention of this provision is an offence in terms of which the perpetrator is liable "on conviction to a fine not exceeding R15 million or imprisonment for a period not exceeding 10 years, or to both a fine and such imprisonment."[261]

Unlisted investments which have received significant attention in South Africa, are over-the-counter (OTC) derivatives. As in other G20 jurisdictions, activity in this area in South Africa can be traced back to the G20 Leader's Statement following the Summit held in Pittsburgh from

---

See Roy Cokayne: Action Groups Mobilise to Recoup R4.5 billion. https://www.iol.co.za/business-report/companies/action-groups-mobilise-to-recoup-r45-billion-13902758 (last visited 13 June 2019).

255 GNR 98 of 9 February 2018 (Government Gazette 41433). Unlike other jurisdictions, South Africa has the curious situation whereby the regulation of companies and the regulation of listed securities fall under different ministries, namely the Ministry of Trade and Industry and the Ministry of Finance. Fertile ground for regulatory arbitrage.

256 The FMA Regulations will be discussed infra in connection with OTC derivatives and central counterparties.

257 Supra. The FMA and FSRA do not have the same remedies though.

258 Section 3 FSRA.

259 Section 1 FSRA. The Companies Act 71 of 2008 defines a "share" in a standard fashion as "one of the units into which the proprietary interest in a profit company is divided."

260 Section 111 FSRA. The specific financial sector law in the case of offering, promoting, marketing or distribution of an unlisted share appears to be the FAIS Act. See definition of "financial service", "financial services provider" and "intermediary service". The Ombud For Financial Services Providers is reported to have issued determinations against financial advisers who put their clients property into property syndication investments (Sharemax)" about a decade ago. See Martin Hesse: Ombud orders advisers to pay back the money. https://www.iol.co.za/personal-finance/ombud-orders-advisers-to-pay-back-the-money-13601546 (last visited 13 June 2019).

261 Section 266 FSRA.

the 24 to 25 September 2009.[262] In furtherance of the G20 objective, the FMA Regulations were issued on 9 February 2018 in South Africa.[263] The FMA Regulations which are very detailed, bring "OTC derivative providers" firmly into the regulatory framework. They may not "originate, issue or sell OTC derivatives or make a market in OTC derivatives unless they are licensed."[264]

In addition to extending the regulatory framework to the OTC market for derivatives, the FMA Regulations provide a detailed framework for the regulation of central counterparties.[265] This is in line with the statement made by the G20 leaders at the Pittsburgh Summit.[266]

Also in line with the statement by the G20 leaders at the Pittsburgh Summit, the FMA has been amended to provide for the licensing of a trade repository.[267] The FMA Regulations set out additional reporting requirements for OTC derivative providers.[268]

IOSCO recently completed a study on wholesale markets, some of whose activities overlap with OTC derivatives.[269] South Africa had embarked on a Financial Markets Review in which issues of market conduct as it relates to wholesale markets conduct are raised.[270]

(e) Public offers (Companies). The FMA deals extensively with the licensing and operational requirements for exchanges. The fundamental legal

---

262 G20 Leaders Pittsburgh Statement http://www.g20.utoronto.ca/2009/2009communique0925.html. (last visited 13 June 2019): "All standardized OTC derivative contracts should be traded on exchanges or electronic trading platforms, where appropriate, and cleared through central counterparties by end-2012 at the latest. OTC derivative contracts should be reported to trade repositories. Non-centrally cleared contracts should be subject to higher capital requirements."

263 Supra.

264 Section 2 of the FMA Regulations as read with section 6 (8) of the FMA.

265 A central counterparty is a specialised clearing house which interposes itself as the buyer to every seller and the seller to every buyer. Regulation of the generic clearing house is discussed infra.

266 Supra. In respect of central counterparties, the FMA regulations, inter-alia, contain provisions for a risk management framework; general capital requirements; capital calculation for operational risk; capital calculation for credit risk; capital calculation for counterparty risk; capital requirements for the minimum capital required for credit value adjustment (CVA); calculation of a central counterparties credit risk exposure; capital calculation for market risk and liquidity risk.

267 Sections 54 to 58 FMA.

268 Section 8 FMA Regulations.

269 IOSCO Task Force Requirements for Wholesale Market Conduct. https://www.iosco.org/library/pubdocs/pdf/IOSCOPD563.pdf (last visited 13 June 2019).

270 2018 Financial Markets Review supra.

framework regulating offers of securities to the public is still to be found in company law.[271]

Offers of securities to the public cannot be made unless the offeror is a company and the offer is accompanied by a prospectus.[272] Other than in the case of securities that are the subject of a company's initial public offering,[273] primary offers of securities to the public of any listed securities may not be made otherwise than in accordance with the requirements of the relevant exchange. No primary offer to the public of unlisted securities of the company may be made unless the offer is accompanied by a registered prospectus that satisfies the requirements of section 100.[274]

In the case of a primary offer to the public of unlisted securities of a company, no secondary offer of any securities of the company to the public can be made unless the offer is accompanied by a registered prospectus or a written statement that complies with prescribed requirements of the Companies Act.[275]

The extensive requirements of a prospectus as laid down in the Companies Act apply only to listed securities that are the subject of an initial public offering.[276] These requirements are substantially in line with

---

271 Companies Act 71 of 2008 supra.

272 Section 99 (1) and (2) Companies Act.

273 An initial public offering means an offer of securities to the public where no securities of that company have previously been the subject of an offer to the public. Section 95 (e) Companies Act. A rights offer is defined as an offer by an issuer to existing holders of securities to subscribe for further securities in the issuer in proportion to their existing holdings by means of the issue of a renounceable right that is traded as either "fully paid" or "no paid" rights or a non-pronounceable right. (See, for example, "definitions" in the JSE's Listings Requirements). A rights offer therefore falls outside of the definition of initial public offering.

274 Section 99 (3) (a) Companies Act. Section 100 Of the Companies Act is discussed infra.

275 Section 99 as read with section 101 of the Companies Act.

276 Sections 100–102 Companies Act. The requirements for prospectuses are extensive and must, inter-alia: include all the information that an investor may reasonably require to assess the assets and liabilities, financial position, profits and losses, cash flow and prospects of the company in which the investor proposes to acquire an interest; state the date of registration of the prospectus; have attached to it copies of any material agreement as prescribed or in the case of an unwritten agreement, a memorandum giving full particulars of the agreement; not contain a statement that the whole or any portion of the issue of the securities offered to the public has been or is being underwritten, unless a copy of the underwriting agreement has been filed; not name any person as a director or a prospective director of the company unless the director or proposed director has consented in writing; not include any statement made by an expert or reference to any statement purported to be made by an expert unless the expert has consented in writing to the

IOSCO Principle 16 which provides that issuers should make "full, accurate and timely disclosure of financial results, risk and other information which is material to an investor's decisions."

A company must not vary or agree to vary any material terms of an agreement referred to in the prospectus within a year after the date of the filing of the prospectus, other than in the ordinary course of business. A variation may only be made where it was contemplated in the prospectus or it is authorised or ratified by an ordinary resolution adopted at a general shareholders meeting.[277]

In the case where securities are offered to the public in terms of a prospectus, every:

i. person who becomes a director between the issuing of the prospectus and the holding of the first annual general meeting at which directors are elected or appointed;
ii. person who has consented to be named in the prospectus as a director, or as having agreed to become a director either immediately or after an interval of time;
iii. promoter of the company; or
iv. person who authorised or is regarded as having authorised the issue of the prospectus or made the offer to the public

is liable to compensate any person who acquires securities on the faith of the prospectus for any loss or damage the person may have sustained as a result of any untrue statement in the prospectus, or in any report or memorandum appearing on the face of the prospectus.[278]

(f) Public offers (Collective Investment Schemes)

Offers to the public to invest in collective investment schemes are governed by CISCA, which provides that before entering into a transaction with an investor, information about the investment objectives of the collective investment scheme, the calculation of the net asset value and dealing prices, charges, risk factors and distribution of income accruals must be disclosed to the investor. In addition, information that the manager considers necessary to enable the investor to make an informed

statement being used before the prospectus was filed; and not name any person as the auditor, attorney, banker or broker of the company unless it is accompanied by the written consent of the named persons agreeing to be named to act in the said capacity and to the use of that person's name in the prospectus. See also Henochsberg on the Companies Act 71 of 2008, volume 1 page 381 (issue 8).

277 Section 103 Companies Act.

278 Section 104 Companies Act.

decision must be given to the investor timeously and in a comprehensive manner.[279]

The manager of a collective investment scheme is required to ensure that disclosure of any information in respect of a collective investment scheme is fair, consistent, transparent and accurate.[280] In addition, the manager of a CIS is required to disclose in all marketing material that the manager has a right to close the portfolio to new investors in order to manage it more efficiently in accordance with its mandate.[281]

A CIS manager is required to publish quarterly on its website, a general investor report, available to investors on request, which details:

i. the number of participatory interests;
ii. net asset value per participatory interest;
iii. an analysis of the portfolio with reference to the extent to which it has or has not adhered to its policy objective;
iv. total expense ratio applicable to the portfolio;
v. a statement of changes in the composition of the portfolio during the reporting period; and
vi. any additional information relevant to the portfolio, taking into account the requirements for the minimum disclosure document ("MDD").[282]

A CIS manager is required to produce an MDD for each portfolio administered under its CIS. The manager must use the MDD for purposes of disclosing information to an investor before entering into a transaction with an investor and for purposes of providing a general investor report to its investors. A manager must, inter-alia, ensure that each MDD:

i. sets out the essential characteristics of a portfolio to enable investors to understand the nature and risks of the portfolio and to make informed investment decisions;
ii. is in the prescribed format (i.e. it does not contain the unnecessary technical jargon);

279 Section 3 CISCA.

280 Section 15 BN 92 of 8 August 2014: Advertising, Marketing and Information Disclosure Requirements for Collective Investment Schemes (Government Gazette 37895 – "CIS Information Disclosure Requirements").

281 Section 15 CIS Information Disclosure Requirements.

282 Section 15 (5) CIS Information Disclosure Requirements. The MDD is a short document containing key information pertaining to a portfolio or scheme that a manager provides to an investor to assist the investor in understanding the CIS product.

iii. is no longer than 2 double sided or 4 one-sided pages of A4 sized paper and is set in readable characters or fonts, spacing and format; and

iv. contains a statement that it is the MDD.[283] An MDD is required to disclose at least the prescribed information.[284]

IOSCO's principles have a requirement for disclosure that is sufficient to enable an investor to evaluate the suitability of an investment in a CIS and the basis for asset valuation, pricing and redemption.[285] The CIS disclosure requirements for CISs in South Africa are largely in line with the IOSCO principles.

A person who contravenes CISCA, in the circumstances is liable to certain penalties.[286]

There are additional legal requirements in the case of CISIPs. A manager of a CISIP "must apply for permission for such participating interests to be dealt with on an exchange."[287] CISCA provides that Part D of Chapter 2 of the Companies Act (dealing with capitalisation of profit companies) applies to the repurchase of a participatory interest by a CISIP. CISCA

283 Section 16 (3) (a) to (e) CIS Information Disclosure Requirements.

284 Section 6 and 16 (mandatory disclosures) for CIS Information. Disclosure Requirements include: the investment objective and a summary of the investment policy of the portfolio as provided for in terms of the supplemental deed and any other mandate that may be narrower than the investment policy; the risk reward profile of the investment, including appropriate guidance on and warnings of the risks associated with investment in the relevant portfolio; the portfolio benchmark where applicable; fees and charges (total expense ratio, management fees, initial fees, performance fees, advisory fees and any other applicable fees) associated with the most expensive class available directly from the manager for investment by members of the public; the portfolio launch or inception date; the portfolio category or classification; the portfolio size; the name of the manager, trustee and/or custodian and their relevant contact details; asset allocation; all prescribed mandatory disclosures; the frequency of publication of prices and where or how prices are published or made available; and where and how to obtain, free of charge, additional information on the proposed investment.

285 IOSCO Principle 26 and 27.

286 Section 107 CISCA. These offenses include disseminating information which he or she knows or ought reasonably to know is false or misleading or is likely or intended to induce another to purchase or deal in a participatory interest; making or publishing any statement or forecast which he or she knows is likely or intended to be misleading, false or deceptive to induce another person to purchase or deal in a participatory interest; or conceals material information at his or her disposal to induce another person to purchase or deal in a participatory interest. In addition, there is civil liability to any other person for any loss or damage suffered by the person as a result of such contravention or failure.

287 Section 50 CISCA.

further provides that the reference to "shares" in that part of the Companies Act, includes participatory interest in a CISIPs.[288]

Taking cognizance of the provisions of CISCA, the JSE Listing Requirements impose the additional condition that "a Deed (including any supplemental deeds) approved by the Registrar of CISs) must comply with the Listing Requirements."[289]

(g) Takeover Code

The activity of investing is dynamic. Investors invest in securities for different purposes. Many investors, including retail and institutional investors, take a long-term view to their investment as they anticipate returns in the form of dividends and capital gain in the case of shares. Institutional investors include pension funds, insurance companies, sovereign wealth funds and hedge funds.

Investors can be passive or active particularly in the case of institutional investors who seek to achieve a particular return on their portfolios in line with their investment mandates. These investors can be active in the sense of closely monitoring the performance of asset managers and even changing them where the performance is regarded as falling below a particular benchmark. Investors can also be active in the sense of seeking to enforce changes in the companies in which they invest through what has become known as "shareholder activism". This is an activity closely associated with hedge funds.[290]

---

288 Section 50 CISCA supra. Part D of the Companies Act Regulates such aspects as the legal nature of shares; the authorisation for shares, preferences, rights, limitations and other terms attaching to shares; the issuing of shares; subscription for shares and considerations therefor; approval for issuing shares in certain cases; options for subscription of securities; and authorisation of distributions by the board.

289 Paragraph 13.32 JSE Listings Requirements. In terms of paragraph 13.33 of the JSE Listings Requirements: "A CISIP is restricted to investment in property shares ... directly in immovable property or such other assets as determined by the CIS Registrar from time to time." Aligning the position of CISIPs with companies, it is further provided that "a CISIP may only issue further participatory interests by way of a rights issue to existing CISIP investors ..." Paragraph 13.34 of the JSE Listings Requirements provides that "in its pre-listing statement/prospectus, a CISIP must also include evidence of registration from the CIS Registrar; and salient provisions of the deed."

290 Shareholder activism has been slow to catch on in South Africa. A sole crusader Theo Botha has been attempting, with limited success, to hold listed companies to account. Asset managers have been accused of failing to fulfil their agency mandates by not voting or voting uncritically with management at annual general meetings. The Government owned Public investment Commission, one of the largest investment managers in South Africa whose primary mandate in the management of the assets of the Government Employees Pension Fund, has forced some progressive changes in corporate governance.

Another category of investor is a share dealer, which can be a professional or a speculator. Such an investor is generally driven by short-term objectives and trends.

Regardless of whatever category an investor falls into, its objectives may be disrupted by the activities of other shareholders in a company that it has invested in. The activities of these other shareholders can be viewed as inconsequential in the case of the acquisition of an insignificant stake in the company depending on the spread of shareholding in the company. On the other hand, the activities of the shareholders may be regarded as aggressive as in the case where the shareholder builds up or seeks to build up a stake in a company which can be deemed to be determinative or potentially determinative of the future of the company.

Policymakers have long recognised that the activities of shareholders with sufficient financial muscle to build up significant stakes in companies, may not always be doing so in the best interests of the wider body of shareholders. In recognition of this danger, company law in South Africa as in other jurisdictions, has imposed certain reporting requirements when shareholders attain certain levels of shareholding in public companies. Where a shareholder in a company acquires a beneficial interest in

> sufficient securities of a class issued by (a) company such that, as a result of the acquisition, the shareholder holds a beneficial interest amounting to 5 per cent, (then) 10 per cent, (then) 15 per cent, or any further whole multiples of 5 per cent, of the issued securities of that class, the shareholder is required to notify the company within 3 business days of the attainment of the threshold of the respective thresholds and further multiples of 5 per cent.[291]

In the case where a shareholder acting alone or in concert with other people acquires voting shares in a public company which exceed the percentage, currently 35 per cent, prescribed by the Minister responsible for companies, such shareholder is required to notify the company within one business day after the vesting of the prescribed percentage. Within 1 month after the notice to the company, the shareholder is required to deliver a written offer known as a mandatory offer, in compliance with the Takeover

---

Some private asset managers e.g. Allan Gray Investments have begun challenging companies on the issue of remuneration. It is a long way however, to the kind of effective activism associated with the likes of Elliot Management. See: Natalie Sherman: Elliott Management: The hedge fund not afraid of a fight. https://www.bbc.com/news/business-39630871 (last visited 13 June 2019).

291 Section 122 of the Companies Act.

Regulations, to the holders (minority shareholders) of the remaining securities of that company to acquire their securities.[292] The value per share of the mandatory offer has to be comparable with the offer for securities made by the offeror to an offeree which resulted in the offeror exceeding the prescribed percentage holding (35 per cent).

If within 4 months after the mandatory offer, such offer is accepted by holders of at least 90 per cent of the securities, excluding shares held before the offer by the offeror, then the provisions of the Companies Act relating to the compulsory acquisition of the remaining shares may be invoked.[293] In these circumstances, the Takeover Regulation Panel[294] may, in terms of its guidelines approve the appointment of an independent expert to prepare a valuation of shares in the acquiree company. The valuation has to be in accordance with "generally accepted valuation approaches and methods in use from time to time". The independent expert's opinion (commonly known as the "fair and reasonable") must, amongst other requirements, confirm that the offer is fair and reasonable and that it has been given to the board of the offeree company for the sole purpose of assisting the board of that company to form and express an opinion for the benefit of the minorities.[295]

(h) Corporate Governance

Corporate governance plays an important role not only in the promotion of a just and ethical society, but in the addition of vital protection for securities holders. A detailed discussion of the status of the implementation of corporate governance principles in South Africa is beyond the scope of this work. However, brief reference will be made to the provisions of the Companies Act, the King IV Corporate Governance Code and exchange listings requirements.

The governance of companies is provided for in chapter 2, Part F of the Companies Act, sections 57 to 78. The Provisions of this Part of the Companies Act contain standard requirements with respect to procedure and conduct of persons responsible for governance of a company.

---

292 Section 123 of the Companies Act. To avoid the mandatory application, it is not uncommon for investment bankers to structure acquisitions in such a way that they do not exceed the threshold of 34, 9 per cent.

293 Section 124 of the Companies Act. This section also sets out actions and time limits, within which an affected minority shareholder, can approach a court for an order that the offeror is not entitled to acquire the minority shareholder's securities or to impose conditions of acquisition which are different from those included in the original offer.

294 Established in terms of section 196 of the Companies Act.

295 Section 90 Companies Regulations, 2011 GN R 351 of 26 April 2011 (Government Gazette 34239) as amended by GN R 619 of 20 August 2013 (Government Gazette 36759) and GN R 82 of 5 February 2014 (Government Gazette 37299).

As a general statement, the business and affairs of a company must be managed by or under the direction of its board, which has the authority to exercise all of the powers and perform any of the functions of the company.[296]

Each director of a "for profit" company must be elected by the persons entitled to exercise voting rights in such an election, to serve for an indefinite term or fixed term.[297]

A director may be removed by an ordinary resolution adopted at a shareholders meeting.[298] Specific requirements are laid down with respect to notice to the director concerned and the affording of an opportunity to the director to make representations.

In the case where a director of a company has a personal interest in respect of a matter to be considered at a meeting of the board, the director:

i. must disclose the interest and its general nature before the matter is considered at the meeting;
ii. must disclose to the meeting any material information relating to the matter, and known to the director;
iii. may disclose any observation or pertinent insights relating to the matter if requested to do so by other directors;
iv. if present at the meeting, must leave the meeting immediately after making any disclosure contemplated in the foregoing paragraphs;
v. must not take part in the consideration of the matter, except to the extent contemplated in the foregoing paragraphs;

296 Section 66 of the Companies Act.

297 Section 68 of the Companies Act. Unless the company's Memorandum of Incorporation provides otherwise, directors are to be elected separately. In other words, the election is to be conducted as a series of votes on the candidacy of a single individual to fill a single vacancy, with the series of votes continuing until all vacancies on the board have been filled. Each share entitled to vote may be cast once for a vacancy which is then filled by the majority of votes for the particular candidate. See Henochsberg on the Companies Act supra, page 264 (3) (issue 18). One would hope that at some point in the not too distant future, some form of cumulative voting will be introduced which would enable shareholders, especially minority shareholders, to elect a director by casting all their votes for a single nominee when there are multiple openings on the board. See SEC Gov. Cumulative voting. https://www.sec.gov/fast-answers/answers-cumulativevotehtm.html (last visited 13 June 2019).

298 Section 71 of the Companies Act.

vi. must not execute any document on behalf of the company in relation to the matter, unless specifically requested or directed to do so by the board.[299]

A director of a company must not use his or her position as a director to gain a personal advantage or knowingly cause harm to the company. The director must communicate to the board at the earliest practicable opportunity, any information coming to his or her attention unless the director reasonably believes that the information is immaterial to the company, is generally available to the public or known to the other directors or the director is bound by a legal or ethical obligation of confidentiality. When the director is acting in the capacity of a director, he or she:

i. must exercise good faith and for a proper purpose;
ii. in the best interests of the company; and
iii. with the degree of care, skill and diligence that may reasonably be expected of a person carrying out the same functions in relation to the company as those carried out by that director; and having the general knowledge, skill and experience of that director.

To satisfy the requirement that the director has acted in the best interests of the company or exercised the necessary degree of care, skill and diligence, the director will have to demonstrate that he or she has taken reasonably diligent steps to become informed about the matter; has no personal interest in the subject matter of the decision or made the required disclosures; and has made or supported a decision on a rational basis in the best interests of the company. In coming to his or her decision, the director is entitled to rely on the information, opinions, reports or statements provided by employees of the company which the director reasonably believed to be reliable and competent in the functions performed or persons to whom the board may reasonably have delegated the authority or duty to perform a function of the board; and any information, opinions, recommendations, reports or statements, including financial statements and other financial data prepared or presented by the employees or persons to whom authority has been delegated.[300]

A director of a company may, amongst other specified instances, be liable in accordance with the principles of common law relating to breach of a fiduciary duty for any loss or damages sustained by the company as a consequence of failure by the director to make the requisite disclosure

299 Section 75 (5) Companies Act. The seminal case on conflict of interest in South Africa if Robinson v Randfontein Estates Gold Mining Company 1921 AD 168.

300 Section 76 Companies Act.

of financial interests, use by the director of his or her position to gain a personal advantage, knowingly causing harm to the company or failing to act in good faith and in the best interests of the company. A director of a company may also be liable under common law for loss to the company as a result of delict or tort in specified circumstances.[301]

In addition to the provisions of the Companies Act, the practice of adopting corporate governance codes is advancing to the state of general application to companies and public entities. One of the codes cited most frequently in global circles is the G20/OECD's Principles of Corporate Governance.[302] The relevant code in South Africa is the King Code of Corporate Governance, which is a set of voluntary principles and leading practices. It was first published as King 1 on 29 November 1994.[303] It is now in its fourth edition and is known as King IV.[304] The latest edition contains 17 principles, trimmed down from 75 in the third edition. All the King Codes have, amongst other aims, been concerned with the role and responsibilities of the governing body of a company or public entity and its interaction with management and other material stakeholders.[305]

---

301 Section 77 Companies Act.

302 G20/OECD Principles of Corporate Governance. http://www.oecd.org/corporate/principles-corporate-governance.htm (last visited 13 June 2019).

303 The Institute of Directors in Southern Africa (IoDSA) established in July 1993 the King Committee on Corporate Governance. The King Committee produced the first King Report on Corporate Governance which was published 29 November 1994. https://www.iodsa.co.za/page/kingIII (last visited 13 June 2019).

304 King Code on Corporate Governance for South Africa. https://c.ymcdn.com/sites/www.iodsa.co.za/resource/resmgr/king_iv/King_IV_Report/IoDSA_King_IV_Report_-_WebVe.pdf (last visited 13 June 2019).

305 The stated objectives of King IV are to: promote corporate governance as integral to running an organisation and delivering governance outcomes such as an ethical culture performance, effective control and legitimacy; broaden the acceptance of King IV by making it accessible and fit for implementation across a variety of sectors and organisational types; reinforce corporate governance as a holistic and interrelated set of arrangements to be understood and implemented in an integrated manner; encourage transparent and meaningful reporting to stakeholders; and present corporate governance as concerned not only with structure and process, but also ethical consciousness and conduct. The underpinning philosophy of King IV is sustainable development. This is understood as a development that meets the needs of the present without compromising the ability of future generations to meet their needs. In addition, sustainable development is regarded as a primary ethical and economic imperative and is a fitting response to the organisation being an integral part of society as well as its status as a corporate citizen meeting its stakeholders needs, interests and expectations.

Although King IV is a set of voluntary principles, the listings requirements of the JSE, for instance, mandate the implementation of specific corporate governance practices taken from the "the King Code".[306]

(g) Audit

An integral aspect of corporate governance and the protection that it affords to investors is the requirement for accurate financial information. In practice, the only meaningful way that financial information can be assured is through the statutory audit.

The audit profession in South Africa is governed by the Independent Regulatory Board for Auditors (IRBA), which, like the FSCA and NT, falls under the jurisdiction of the Ministry of Finance.[307]

Every company must keep accurate and complete accounting records. It is specifically provided that it is an offence for a company to fail to keep accurate or complete accounting records or to falsify any of the accounting records with the intention to deceive or mislead any person. It is also an offence for any person to falsify a company's accounting records.[308]

---

306 Paragraph 3.84, 7.F.5 and 22/15(h) of the JSE Listings Requirements provides for instance, that: there must be a policy evidencing a clear balance of power and authority at board of directors level, to ensure that no one director has unfettered powers of decision-making; the Chief Executive Officer and the chairperson are not the same person; the issuer has audit, remuneration and social and ethics committees; brief CVs of each director are provided in respect of each new listing. CVs of each director standing for election or re-election at the general meeting should accompany the notice of the general meeting; the capacity of each director is to be categorised executive, non-executive or independent using specified guidelines; all issuers must have an executive financial director; and the audit committee must on an annual basis, satisfy itself of the appropriateness of the expertise and experience of the financial director; ensure that the issuer has established appropriate financial reporting procedures; that those procedures are operating; and request from the audit firm a list of all applicant issuers which are its clients.

307 In terms of section 4 of the Auditing Professions Act 26 of 2005, the functions of IRBA are, inter alia, to take steps to promote the integrity of the auditing profession (including investigating alleged improper conduct); conducting disciplinary hearings; imposing sanctions for improper conduct; and conducting practice reviews or inspections; take steps it considers necessary to protect the public in their dealings with registered auditors; prescribing standards of professional competence, ethics and conduct of registered auditors; encouraging education in connection with, and research into, any matter affecting the auditing profession; and prescribing auditing standards.

308 Section 214 Companies Act. In the case of a listed company, this is made a specific offence in terms of section 81 of the FMA. See FSCA v Harmony. https://www.fsca.co.za/Enforcement-Matters/Documents/EC_Signed%20Judgment_Harmony%20Gold%20Mining%20Company%20Limited_2018-10-04.pdf (last visited 13 June 2019).

The Companies Act sets out specific requirements for a company's annual financial statements.[309]

Each year, a company is required to prepare annual financial statements within 6 months after the end of its financial year. In the case of a public company, the statements must be audited and set out relevant factors including annual turnover; size of workforce and the nature and extent of its activities.[310]

Every public company is required, upon its incorporation, to appoint an auditor. In order to be appointed as an auditor of a company, the person or firm concerned must be a registered auditor and must not be a director or prescribed officer of the company or other person, as described, with a close relationship to the company.[311]

An individual may not serve as the auditor or designated auditor of a company for more than 5 consecutive financial years. In the case where an individual has served as the auditor or designated auditor of a company for 2 or more consecutive financial years, and then ceases to be an auditor or designated auditor, that person may not be appointed again as the auditor or designated auditor of the company until at least a further 2 financial years have elapsed.[312]

At each annual general meeting, a public company must elect an audit committee comprising at least 3 members. Each member of an audit committee must be a director of the company; must not be involved in the day-to-day management of the company's business; be a prescribed officer

---

309 Section 28 Companies Act provides that the statements must satisfy the applicable financial reporting standards as to form and content; present fairly the state of affairs and business of the company, and explain the transactions and financial position of the business of the company; show the company's assets, liabilities and equity, as well as its income and expenses, and any other prescribed information; set out the date on which the statements were published, and the accounting records to which the statements apply; and place on the first page of the statements, a prominent notice indicating whether the statements have been audited in accordance with the requirements of the Companies Act, and if not audited whether they have been independently reviewed; state the name and professional designation of the individual who prepared or supervised the preparation of the statements.

310 Section 30 Companies Act.

311 Section 90 Companies Act.

312 Section 92 Companies Act. The concept of auditor firm rotation was not readily embraced by the profession in South Africa. See Director and Auditor Rotation in South Africa. http://www.mondaq.com/southafrica/x/590796/Audit/Director+and+auditor+rotation+in+South+Africa (last visited 13 June 2019).

or full-time employee of the company; or be a material supplier or customer of the company.[313]

King IV contains recommendations which support and supplement the provisions in the Companies Act. For instance, principle 8 states that "the governing body should ensure that its arrangements for delegation within its own structures promotes independent judgement and assists the balance of power and the effective discharge of its duties." King IV recommends that the role of the audit committee should be to provide independent oversight of the effectiveness of the organisation's assurance functions and services and the integrity of the annual financial statements.[314]

The FMA, as with King IV, prescribes complementary requirements for the appointment by regulated entities, including exchanges, of auditors; the maintenance of accounting records and audit; the functions of an auditor; and the furnishing of information in good faith by the auditor. The registrar is authorised, at any time, by written notice to direct a regulated entity to have its accounts, records and financial statements audited.[315]

Stock exchanges also have complementary provisions for the accreditation and appointment of auditors and reporting accountants, their roles and responsibilities, applicable auditing standards, continuing requirements and modified auditors' reports.[316]

(i). Financial Markets Infrastructures

i. Clearing

In securities markets, clearing is the process of establishing settlement positions, including the calculation of net positions, and the process of checking that securities, cash or both are available for the settlement of obligations. In the case of derivatives, clearing has come to refer to the process of daily marking to market, netting and daily settlement of positions leading to the establishment of final delivery positions in cash,

313 Section 94 Companies Act.

314 Paragraph 51 King IV.

315 Sections 89 to 93 FMA.

316 E.g. JSE Listings Requirements supra. A number of audit firms including KPMG and Nkonki Inc have faced a private and public backlash owing to various instances of unethical conduct. The sanctions have not to date been as severe as the sanction imposed on PwC by the Securities and Exchange Board of India as a consequence of its involvement with the Satyam scandal. See Live Mint: Satyam case: Sebi bans PwC entities from auditing listed firms for two years. https://www.livemint.com/Companies/KlbBm6VhxhQQswdgT9bycK/Satyam-case-Sebi-bans-PwC-entities-from-auditing-listed-fir.html (last visited 13 June 2019).

commodities or securities.[317] In summary, clearing can be described as the process utilised for managing the risk of open positions.[318] The requirements with which an applicant for a clearinghouse licence must comply are set out in the FMA,[319] which sets out additional requirements respecting the functions of a licenced clearinghouse.[320]

ii. Settlement Services and Payment Systems

Settlement is the completion of a transaction in terms of which the seller transfers securities to the buyer and the buyer transfers cash to the seller.[321] The FMA defines "settle" in respect of listed securities as the transfer of a security and the payment of funds or any other consideration payable in respect of the transaction through a settlement system. Settlement in respect of listed derivative instruments, is defined as the completion of

---

317 Section 48 FMA. An independent clearinghouse is defined as one that clears transactions in securities on behalf of any person in accordance with its clearinghouse rules. An associated clearinghouse on the other hand, is defined as one that clears transactions in securities on behalf of an exchange of. Section 1 FMA.

318 Peter Norman: The Risk Controllers (glossary). ISBN 978-0-470-68632-4. This description is in line with the definition of "clear" in section 1 FMA. This part of the study deals with the licensing and operation of clearinghouses in general including central counterparties which have additional requirements as discussed in the context of OTC derivatives supra.

319 Section 8 FMA Regulations. Inter alia, it must demonstrate that it has sufficient assets and resources; it's governance arrangements are clear and transparent; it promotes the safety and efficiency of the clearinghouse, and supports the stability of the broader financial system; it's fit and proper requirements, as prescribed by the registrar, are met; that it complies with the requirements for clearing transactions in securities as prescribed by the registrar; that it has an effective and reliable infrastructure to facilitate the clearing of securities cleared by the clearinghouse; that it has implemented effective arrangements to manage the material risks associated with the operation of a clearinghouse; that it has made arrangements for security and backup procedures to ensure the integrity of the records of transactions cleared through the clearinghouse; and, that in the case of an application for an independent clearinghouse licence, it has made arrangements for the efficient and effective supervision of clearing members.

320 Section 50 FMA. The requirements include the provision of an appropriate infrastructure for clearing of securities; the duty to inform the registrar of any matter that it reasonably believes may pose systemic risk to the financial markets; disclosing to the registrar information about the exposures a clearing member underwrites with the clearinghouse; appropriate arrangements to ensure it has efficient and timely access to funds and assets held as collateral for the due performance of the obligations of clearing members; the issuance of clearing house rules and; enforcement of the clearinghouse rules; supervision of compliance by its clearing members with the clearinghouse rules and directives; supervision of compliance with the FMA by its clearing members; and notification to the registrar as soon as it commences any insolvency proceedings. Section 53 of the FMA sets out additional requirements with which a clearing house rules must comply.

321 Peter Norman: The Risk Controllers supra.

a transaction by the fulfilment of all contractual obligations associated with the resultant position in the instrument.[322] The function of settlement is normally carried out by a central securities depository (CSD). An applicant for a CSD licence as well as a licensed CSD must comply with the requirements of Section 28 of the FMA.[323] Section 25 of the FMA sets out the requirements with which the rules of a CSD must comply.[324]

---

322 Section 1 FMA.

323 The CSD is required to demonstrate that : it has assets and resources in South Africa, including financial, management and human resources with appropriate experience, to perform the functions of a CSD; it has clear and transparent governance arrangements which promote the safety and efficiency of the CSD, and support the stability of the broader financial system; the prescribed fit and proper requirements are met by the applicant or the CSD; arrangements have been made for the efficient and effective monitoring of compliance by participants with the depository rules; it enforces the depository rules and depository directives; it informs the authority of any matter it reasonably believes may give rise to, or increased systemic risk; may issue depository directives; maintains a central securities account with due regard to the interests of the participant and its clients; it may hold all securities of the same kind deposited with it by a participant collectively in a separate central securities account; it notifies a participant in writing of an entry made into the central securities account for the relevant person; it administers and maintains a record of uncertificated securities deposited with it; that on request it will disclose to the authority information about the securities held in a central securities account; it has established and maintains effective, efficient and sustainable infrastructure to perform the functions for which it is licensed; it will notify the authority as soon as it commences an insolvency proceeding. "Participant" is defined in section 1 of the FMA as a person authorised by a licensed CSD to perform custody and administration services or settlement services or both in terms of the depository rules. The duties of participants are set out in section 32 of the FMA.

324 These requirements include: provision of the manner in which transactions in securities settled through the CSD must be settled; provision for equitable criteria for authorisation and exclusion of participants; the provision for requirements in respect of a participant's financial soundness and valid financial cover in respect of actual and potential liabilities, conditional and contingent liabilities; and liabilities which existed before or accrued after a person has ceased to be a participant; provision for requirements in respect of corporate actions; the requirement that a participant, upon written request from a client to withdraw securities held in the securities account must deliver a certificate evidencing the same number of securities or securities of the same nominal value and of the same kind as those held in behalf of the client; provision for requirements in respect of the same day debit balances and prohibit debit balances at the end of a day in a securities account; provision for the purposes and processes by which a CSD may issue depository directives; provision for the manner in which a participant must hold and administer securities; provision for netting arrangements if transactions in one or more categories of securities settled through the CSD settle on a net basis; and provision for the manner in which the CSD monitors compliance by its participants with the FMA.

Securities are bought and sold through a stock exchange or in direct transactions between buyers and sellers. Payment for securities goes hand in hand with transfer of ownership. CSDs[325] are responsible for the settlement of securities in South Africa. The CSD determines the interbank payment obligations arising from these transactions and then refers them for settlement to the only settlement system in use, namely the South African Multiple Option Settlement (SAMOS). SAMOS was developed by the South African Reserve Bank (SARB) to align domestic interbank settlement practices with international best practice. SAMOS, which was designed for large-value interbank transactions as well as retail and securities transactions, is an automated interbank settlement system for banks to settle their interbank obligations on a real-time gross basis, or under a delayed gross settlement arrangement. The SAMOS system is linked to the various participant banks, clearing systems and operators.[326]

Part B – Supervision

1 *Introduction*

It is a fact that many jurisdictions which have embarked on significant regulatory reform programmes have attributed their efforts in this respect to the damage which the GFC inflicted on their respective economies. In the Red Book,[327] the NT as the policymaker stated that;

> the South African financial sector did not experience the financial upheaval seen in advanced economies and, as a result, the economy is in a favourable situation to recover from the downturn and emerge stronger than before.

The NT re-states what has become conventional wisdom to the effect that the financial sector cannot seriously be expected to regulate itself. Therefore, the "light touch" approach to regulation assiduously applied by the likes of Alan Greenspan, former Federal Reserve Chairman, had no future in financial regulation.[328] It was observed that regulators around the world have adopted "a

325 There are now 2 CSDs licensed in South Africa, namely Strate (Pty) in which the JSE is a substantial shareholder, and the newcomer Granite (Pty) Ltd.

326 CPSS Redbook: Payment, Clearing and Settlement Systems in South Africa. https://www.bis.org/cpmi/publ/d105_za.pdf (last visited 13 June 2019).

327 A Safer Financial Sector to Serve South Africa Better ibid page 13.

328 Ibid. Page 13 Red Book.

tougher and more inclusive approach towards supervision" and that the "mandates of regulators and the quality of supervision have been strengthened."[329] In the circumstances, and in view of the need for higher economic growth and job creation, NT stated that:

> it is imperative to ensure that the South African financial system remains competitive and that it is made safer through regulation that follows global best practice but bearing in mind the specific circumstances of our own economy.[330]

Amongst the 15 guiding principles for regulatory reform set out in the Red Book, are statements that "regulation should be risk based, where appropriate, and proportional to the nature scale and complexity of risks present in a regulated entity and the system as a whole." There is also a statement that "the quality of supervision must be sufficiently intense intrusive and effective."[331]

2 *Risk Based Supervision – Context*

In the new regulatory regime in South Africa which is set out in the FSRA, the Authority is enjoined to "have regard to international regulatory and supervisory standards" set by relevant standard setters.[332] In the case of securities, the relevant standard setter is IOSCO.

The responsibilities of securities supervisors encompass intermediaries including brokers, markets, exchanges and other market infrastructures and collective investment schemes. Securities supervision differs in a number of respects from other sectors such as banking and insurance. For example, in South Africa as in other jurisdictions, the self-regulatory model is acknowledged as a valuable complement to the Authority's objective of achieving an appropriate level of securities supervision. Further, securities supervisors place great importance on ensuring that investors are provided with the information necessary to make informed investment decisions on an ongoing basis. As a result, full, timely and accurate disclosure of current and reliable information which is material to investment decisions is critical. Securities regulators also emphasise disclosure by brokers/intermediaries to their clients on matters including investment risk and conflicts of interest.[333]

329 Ibid. Page 24 Red Book.

330 Ibid. Page 4 Red Book.

331 Ibid. Page 25 Red Book.

332 Section 59 (5) (C) FSRA.

333 The Joint Forum CORE PRINCIPLES CROSS-SECTORAL COMPARISON Nov 2001. https://www.bis.org/publ/joint03.pdf page 2.

As indicated in the preceding paragraph, supervision in the securities sector addresses more than just intermediaries (broker-dealers and investment advisors). Consequently, it is important to understand that whereas supervisors in the banking and insurance industries deal almost entirely with the supervision of firms, securities supervisors exercise a much broader scope of jurisdiction. For instance, it is commonly understood that the securities sector as a whole is sensitive to macroeconomic factors. This is owing to the fact that there is typically a predictable correlation between macroeconomic indicators and market sentiment. It follows therefore, that extreme macroeconomic conditions tend to lead to rapid changes in confidence which can, for example, lead to runs on assets by fund managers or rapid unwinding of futures positions which leverage on equity values.[334]

In addition to the features discussed above, there are unique aspects of the securities sector, including Self-Regulatory Organisations (SROs), which are reflected in the IOSCO Principles.[335] Securities regulators may look to SROs to regulate some of the activities of market participants. In some jurisdictions much of the inspection and supervision of entities engaged in securities activity is done by SROs, which are also primarily responsible for market surveillance and for rule enforcement with respect to their members.[336]

IOSCO has developed self-assessment methodologies aimed at implementation. As a first step it has developed a high-level self-assessment methodology for the implementation of the IOSCO Principles by having members complete a self-assessment. More detailed self-assessment methodologies on specific sections of the principles are currently being undertaken.[337]

It should be noted that the banking, insurance and securities sectors all consider customer protection and systemic stability as objectives of the supervisory system. Basel places its greatest emphasis on systemic stability and the IAIS on the customer (in this case, policyholder) protection. IOSCO on the other hand has a more inclusive approach. It emphasises equally its three objectives namely investor protection, fair, transparent and efficient markets and reduction of systemic risk. IOSCO places additional responsibility

334 Joint Forum ibid. page 11.

335 IOSCO Principle 9 reads: "Where the regulatory system makes use of SROs that exercise some direct oversight responsibility for their respective areas of competence, such SROs should be subject to the oversight of the Regulator and should observe standards of fairness and confidentiality when exercising powers and delegated responsibilities."

336 The Joint Forum ibid. page 12. See discussion under … in relation to the view of South African policy makers on the continuing role of SROs.

337 The Joint Forum ibid. page 6. IOSCO has also developed an online self-assessment questionnaire. https://www.iosco.org/online-methodology-2017/ (last visited 13 June 2019).

on supervisors to detect and deter market abuses and fraud. Monitoring and detection involve the use of market surveillance, which is unique to the securities sector. Securities supervisors and, where applicable, SROs are responsible for monitoring trading in listed securities to determine whether there is evidence of securities law violations.[338] While supervisors in banking, insurance and securities all have the authority to investigate possible violations and take legal action against supervised institutions and associated individuals, securities supervisors also have wider authority to take action against non-supervised entities and individuals for violations of securities laws.[339]

Traditionally, supervisors applied a rules-based compliance inclined system that relied on review of transactions and historical performance, covering all operational areas regardless of any demonstrated or probable weakness. Results were evaluated with little emphasis on systemic controls or risk management. It was subsequently realized that rule-based supervision was not an effective tool for preventing financial crises. This realization has led to the emergence of the risk-based approach to supervision where emphasis is placed on process rather than on individual transactions. In this vein, the regulated entity's treatment is based on its risk profile and ability to manage the risk. Risk-based supervision has gained wide acceptance as the majority of supervisors in significant financial centres around the world, including South Africa, now employ some form of risk-based supervision.[340]

Risk-based supervision aims to promote transparency, provide early warning signals and encourage the regulated entities to self-evaluate their position at regular intervals. The risk profile of each regulated entity determines the supervisory programme comprising off-site surveillance, targeted on-site inspections, external audits and regulatory actions as warranted. The process of risk-based supervision involves continuous monitoring and evaluation of the risk profiles of regulated entities in relation to their business strategies and exposures.[341]

A risk-based approach incentivises regulated entities to manage their own risks. Regulators should be able to assess the regulated entities capacity to manage their risks and determine the extent to which this could have an impact on the regulatory objectives of financial stability, investor protection and the

338 The Joint Forum ibid. pages 2 and 13.

339 See: The Executive Officer: Financial Services Board vs Dynamic Wealth Limited and Others supra.

340 Guidelines to Emerging Market Regulators Regarding Requirements for Minimum Entry and Continuous Risk-Based Supervision of Market Intermediaries Final Report. Page 10 http://www.iosco.org/library/pubdocs/pdf/IOSCOPD314.pdf (last visited 13 June 2019).

341 Ibid. Page 10.

upholding of market integrity. Regulators have to make subjective judgments based on the outcomes of these assessments and thus be able to determine where and how to prioritize their supervisory efforts.[342]

In addressing the risk factors relating to the regulated entities for assessment purposes, regulators consider, inter alia, the probability and impact of these factors. Relevant risk factors include the regulated entity's significant activities, inherent risks and internal controls (e.g. quality of risk management procedures and oversight functions). An effective risk assessment model uses both quantitative and qualitative risk assessment tools in order to arrive at a regulated entity's overall risk profile. Data sources include statutory regulatory returns, external and internal auditors' reports, audit reports received from exchanges, self-assessment questionnaires and publicly available information.

A planned risk assessment model captures both qualitative and quantitative factors. The qualitative factors generally take into account the effectiveness of compliance, risk management, internal audit functions and board and senior management oversight. Quantitative factors may include elements of financial analysis including consideration of institutional level protections (earnings, capital and liquidity). The approach to risk-based supervision, in general, emphasizes the identification, classification and categorization of the risks that the institutions are exposed to and the risk management capacity in the overall assessment of the risk along with the determination of the probability and weighting of the major risks for each institution.[343]

The IOSCO Principles require market authorities to monitor large exposures on a market and to share information with one another to permit appropriate assessment of risk.[344] Market authorities must establish trigger levels appropriate to their markets and continuously monitor the size of positions.[345]

When regulators set capital requirements (regulatory capital) for the entities they supervise, such requirements should reflect the risks undertaken by the entities. The IOSCO core principles expressly state that the capital requirements should be risk-based.[346]

For banks, supervisors are expected to establish capital requirements including defining eligible capital components that are at least as strict as the requirements of the Basel Accord. IOSCO and IAIS, by contrast, expect

342 Ibid. Page 10.
343 Ibid. Page 14.
344 Principle 37.
345 The Joint Forum ibid. page 19.
346 The Joint Forum ibid. page 19.

supervisors to promulgate capital requirements but do not have a single international capital framework for their respective sectors.[347]

The results of the overall risk assessment along with probability are used to assign an overall risk rating or risk scoring for each institution. In general, the risk rating is determined as "Impact x Probability". While Impact rating depends on the size and the total assets of the institution, probability generally depends on the risk factors and the associated weights.[348]

Regulators maximize utility of their limited resources with the aim of allocating commensurate attention to the regulated entities. This regulatory attention ranges from requirements including the number and types of statutory reports to be filed, priority for off-site and on-site supervision and ongoing supervisory requirements. In the case where inspection powers are shared between the regulator and an SRO, there is a need to coordinate supervisory resources and schedules. If the SRO has a different risk assessment mechanism from the regulator, coordination and sharing of information should ensure that the inspection approach of the regulator and the SRO are effective and efficient for the mutually-supervised entities.[349]

The total risk score or composite risk rating of a regulated entity should be used to schedule the frequency of inspections for that entity. Inspection planning and inspection execution processes take into account the results of the risk assessment to determine the scope and focus of the inspection. Inspection checklists are used to ensure consistency of the areas inspected and are adapted to suit the risks and specific objectives of each inspection.[350]

3 *Regulatory Framework for Supervision*

To recap, South Africa is still in a transformation phase during which it is moving to a full-scale twin peaks financial services regulatory model. FSRA came into effect on 18 April 2018 and is the overarching legislation for financial services. The introduction of legislation such as FSRA practically necessitates a period of transition in which the new legislation operates side-by-side with existing legislation. Hence, FSRA's objects[351] are restated to encompass all the

347 The Joint Forum ibid. page 19.

348 The Joint Forum ibid. page 10.

349 The Joint Forum ibid. page 20.

350 The Joint Forum ibid.

351 Section 7 FSRA: "the object of this Act is to ... (establish)... in conjunction with the specific financial sector laws, a regulatory and supervisory framework that promotes (a) financial stability; (b) the safety and soundness of financial institutions; (c) the fair and efficient protection of financial customers; (d) the efficiency and integrity of the financial

themes for regulatory reform discussed in the introductory section of this work in the context of the relevant policy documents such as the Red Book.

Anticipating inconsistencies between FSRA and other financial sector laws,[352] FSRA provides that in the event of an inconsistency between FSRA and any financial sector act (as defined) the provisions of FSRA are to prevail. The same applies where there are inconsistencies in the regulations issued under FSRA and regulations issued under any financial sector act.[353]

In this vein, the FMA, FAIS and CISCA contain similar provisions to the effect that unless FSRA states otherwise, the powers and duties of an authority in terms the financial sector law which it administers are additional to the powers and duties which that authority has in terms of FSRA.[354]

FSRA makes it clear that no person may provide a financial product, financial service or market infrastructure as a business or part of its business except in terms of a specific financial sector law.[355]

As part of a relevant authority's off-site supervision, it is empowered to request any person, on notice, to supply the authority with specified information or documents under that person's control which is relevant to assisting the responsible authority to perform its functions in terms of a financial sector law. A supervised or regulated entity receiving such a notice is required to comply with its requirements.[356]

A financial sector regulator is authorised to conduct a supervisory on-site inspection at the business premises of the supervised entity provided it has given prior notice to the supervised entity. The legitimate purpose for which a financial sector regulator may conduct an on-site inspection can be in order to check compliance with a financial sector law; determining the extent of risk posed by the supervised entity in respect of contraventions of a financial sector law; and assisting the financial sector regulator to supervise the relevant financial institution.[357]

The NT is required to establish and maintain the "Financial Sector Information Register", which is a database. The stated purpose of the register database is to provide reliable access to accurate, authoritative and up-to-date

system; (e) the prevention of financial crime; (f) financial inclusion; (g) transformation of the financial sector; and (h a) confidence in the financial system.

352 Other financial sector laws are set out in Schedule 1 of the FSRA, and include the FMA, FAIS, and CISCA.

353 Section 9 FSRA.

354 Section 1A (3) FMA, section 1A (2) FAIS and section 1A (2) CISCA.

355 Section 111 (1) FSRA supra.

356 Section 131 FSRA.

357 See section 132 FSRA.

information relating to financial sector laws, regulations, regulatory instruments and their implementation.[358]

The FMA, FAIS and CISCA contain supervisory provisions which are substantially consistent with the provisions FSRA.[359]

The supervisory responsibility of regulators in securities extends beyond intermediaries and brokers to the markets. Off-site and on-site supervision also apply to market infrastructures including exchanges, although the information requirements are likely to be more extensive in view of the nature of the operations of market infrastructures. Of necessity, the supervision of exchanges has to be more intrusive, hence the requirement for exchanges to "have made arrangements for the efficient and effective surveillance of all transactions effected through the exchange and for the supervision of authorised users so as to identify possible market abuse and ensure compliance with exchange rules and exchange directives and the FMA."[360]

The types of conduct which the capital markets regulators would be on the lookout for in terms of this requirement for surveillance are insider-trading, price manipulation and false statements.[361] For the purposes of the investigation of market abuse, the regulatory authority in South Africa makes use of an in-house department of market abuse which does the legwork in the investigations of market abuse. In between meetings of the directorate of market abuse (directorate), the in-house team meets weekly with the exchanges to review the exchanges surveillance activity for the purposes, inter-alia, of sharing information and collaborating in investigative efforts. The in-house team presents the findings of its investigations to the directorate at its quarterly meetings. Membership of the directorate is drawn from professions and relevant industries including law, accountancy, insurance, banking, fund management, institutional investment, SARB, the Prudential Authority and representatives from each of the exchanges. The duties and powers of the directorate include

358 Section 256 to 258 as read with Schedule 3 (documents to be published in the register).

359 E.g. Sections 1A (6) and 6 (3) FMA; section 1A (5) and (6) FAIS and session 1A (5) and (6) CISCA.

360 Section 8 (d) FMA. This requirement is in line with IOSCO Principle 34: "There should be ongoing regulatory supervision of exchanges and trading systems which should aim to ensure that the integrity of trading is maintained through fair and equitable rules and an appropriate balance between the demands of different market participants.

361 Sections 78 to 81 FMA. Harmony Gold Mining company was recently fined R30 Million for a contravention of section 81 FMA (previously section 76 SSA) making "false, misleading or deceptive statements, promises and forecasts." See FSCA vs Harmony Gold Mining Company Limited Enforcement Committee Case No 35/2017. https://www.fsca.co.za/Enforcement-Matters/Documents/EC_Signed%20Judgment_Harmony%20Gold%20Mining%20Company%20Limited_2018-10-04.pdf (last visited 13 June 2019).

the consideration of the investigation reports of the in-house team and the making of recommendations respecting investigations into the relevant offences.[362] The detection of market abuse in its various forms is challenging. Regulators and SROs charged with the responsibility of surveillance are constrained to invest in electronic surveillance systems which facilitate the monitoring and analysis of trades in securities listed on exchanges. Depending on the size of the exchange in a particular jurisdiction, the sizes of surveillance teams can vary from, say, 1 individual to a much larger complement of individuals. The speed of trading more frequently referred to in the context of "high frequency trading", which is driven primarily by algorithms, adds to the challenges faced by regulators.

4 *Enforcement – Context*

Financial sector regulators in South Africa are required to have regard to international regulatory and supervisory standards as set out by relevant standard setters, i.e. IOSCO.[363] Generally, the enforcement powers of securities regulators, unlike other financial sector regulators, are comprehensive and enable supervisors not only to investigate, but to prosecute and extend their jurisdiction beyond supervised entities to take action against non-supervised entities and individuals for violations of securities laws.[364] Securities violations can also occur both on and off the securities markets.[365]

Another difference from measures normally taken by other financial sector regulators is the securities regulator's preference for transparency in the enforcement process. Investigations conducted by securities supervisors are not usually public, but the enforcement proceedings are generally open to the public. Securities supervisors normally publish the results of proceedings and sanctions imposed to warn or alert customers of particular entities, individuals or schemes.[366] This is because in the securities sector, supervisory transparency and accountability are linked to the maintenance of orderly markets which in turn boosts confidence in the markets. In the view of securities supervisors such transparency strengthens perceptions of regulatory

362 Section 85 FMA. Section 85.

363 Section 58 (5) (see) FSRA supra. Principle 11 of the IOSCO Principles provides that "the Regulator should have comprehensive enforcement powers." Principle 12 of the IOSCO Principles provides that "the regulatory system should ensure an effective and credible use of inspection, investigation, surveillance and enforcement powers and implementation of an effective compliance programme."

364 The Joint Forum ibid. page 3.

365 The Joint Forum ibid. page 2.

366 The Joint Forum ibid. page 14.

predictability. This facilitates normal market functions and improves the credibility of the enforcement process. In addition, transparency contributes to supervisory accountability.[367]

Securities supervisors can recommend that the relevant domestic criminal prosecutors take enforcement actions. Referrals for criminal prosecution are rare in South Africa. Regulators generally pursue the administrative action as provided for in FSRA.[368] The burden of proof required for a finding against the regulated entity or individual against whom proceedings have been brought in administrative proceedings is that of proof on a balance of probabilities. The burden of proof required in the case of criminal proceedings is proof beyond a reasonable doubt, which is much more difficult to achieve.[369]

For the purposes of enforcement, amongst other supervisory requirements, the IOSCO principles recommend that regulators should establish information sharing mechanisms which set out when and how they will share public and non-public information with their domestic and foreign counterparts. The IOSCO principles also recommend that the regulatory system should allow for assistance to be provided to foreign regulators who need to make enquiries into the discharge of their functions and exercise of their powers.[370] In the spirit of cooperation, all full IOSCO members are required to commit themselves to a Multilateral Memorandum of Understanding which is designed to assist regulators with cross-border enforcement enquiries and requirements.[371]

5 *Regulatory Framework for Enforcement*

Wide-ranging regulatory enforcement measures are provided for in FSRA. These measures include:

---

367 The Joint Forum ibid. page 11.

368 Section 167 FSRA. Previously, enforcement matters were referred to the Enforcement Committee in terms of section 97 of the FMA and section 10A of the FSB Act 97 of 1990, both repealed.

369 The last successful criminal prosecution in a securities case was in the *State vs Jeffrey Israel Levenstein*, Appeal Court case 809/12. http://www.justice.gov.za/sca/judgments/sca_2013/sca2013-147.pdf. This case, inter alia, involved insider trading.

370 Principles 13 to 15 IOSCO Principles.

371 Multilateral Memorandum of Understanding concerning Consultation and Cooperation and the Exchange of Information adopted May 2002 and revised May 2012. https://www.iosco.org/library/pubdocs/pdf/IOSCOPD386.pdf. (last visited 13 June 2019). The MMoU will be replaced by the Enhanced Multilateral Memorandum of Understanding (EMMoU) adopted in 2016, in the years to come. https://www.iosco.org/about/pdf/Text-of-the-EMMoU.pdf. (last visited 13 June 2019). The EMMoU which provides, for expanded co-operation amongst regulators, has already been adopted by a number of jurisdictions including British Columbia, Hong Kong, Ontario, Quebec, Singapore, Australia and the United Kingdom.

(a) directives requiring a financial institution to take specified action where for instance, the institution is conducting business in a way that poses a material risk to the efficiency and integrity of capital markets;[372] or
(b) removal of a person from a specified position or function in a financial institution where the person has contravened a financial sector law; been involved in financial crime; or no longer complies with fit and proper requirements.[373]

It is possible for a person to give a written undertaking to the responsible authority respecting that person's future conduct in a matter regulated by a financial sector law. Upon acceptance by the responsible authority, that undertaking becomes enforceable in terms of FSRA. The responsible authority is required to publish each enforceable undertaking that it accepts as well as each variation or withdrawal thereof. Where the person contravenes an enforceable undertaking, the responsible authority may refer the matter to the financial services tribunal (Tribunal).[374]

The responsible authority (e.g. the FSCA) for a financial sector law may institute proceedings against a person in the High Court for an order to ensure compliance with the relevant financial sector law. The High Court may if it appears to it that:
(a) the person is either contravening or proposes contravening a financial sector law;
(b) the person has previously engaged in such conduct; and
(c) there is a danger of substantial irreparable damage or harm if the person contravenes a financial sector law,

make an order as applied for by the responsible authority.[375]

The responsible authority may issue a debarment order to any natural person who has contravened a financial sector law in a material way; contravened an enforceable undertaking in a material way; attempted or conspired with another person to contravene a financial sector law in a material way; or contravened the law of a foreign country that corresponds to a financial sector law in a material way.[376]

The responsible authority for a financial sector law may, by order served on any person, impose an appropriate administrative penalty on that person if the

372 Section 144 FSRA.

373 Section 145 FSRA. This particular remedy is becoming more commonplace. It is provided for in MiFID 2 for instance.

374 Section 151 FSRA. The Tribunal is established in terms of section (219 (1) FSRA discussed infra.

375 Section 152 FSRA.

376 Section 153 FSRA.

person has contravened a financial sector law or contravened an enforceable undertaking accepted by the responsible authority. In determining an appropriate administrative penalty for particular conduct, the responsible authority must have regard, inter-alia, to the need to deter such conduct; whether the person has cooperated with the responsible authority; and any mitigating factors submitted by the person.[377]

The administrative penalty may include an amount for reasonable costs incurred by the responsible authority in connection with the contravention. An administrative action is not competent, where criminal proceedings for the same contravention have been instituted.[378]

An administrative penalty order made by a responsible authority may be made an order of court with the effect of a civil judgement, if the amount payable in terms of the order by the responsible authority has not been paid as required.[379]

In the case of insider trading, an administrative sanction may be ordered which does not exceed:

(a) the profit made or the loss averted as a result of the contravention;
(b) an amount of up to R1 million, adjusted annually to reflect the Consumer Price Index, plus 3 times the profit made, or loss averted;
(c) interest; and
(d) costs incurred by the relevant authority including investigation costs.[380]

An Ombud Council has been established for the purpose of ensuring that financial customers have access to, and are able to use affordable, effective, independent and fair alternative dispute resolution processes for complaints about financial institutions in relation to financial products, financial services, and the services of market infrastructures.[381]

---

377 Section 167 (2) FSRA. The matters which a responsible authority may have regard to include: the nature, duration, seriousness and extent of the convention; any loss or damage suffered by any person as a result of the conduct; the extent of any financial or commercial benefit to the person, or a juristic person related to the person, arising from the conduct; whether the person has previously contravened a financial sector law; the effects of the conduct on the financial system and financial stability; the effect of the proposed penalty on financial stability; and the extent to which the conduct was deliberate or reckless.

378 Section 167 (3) and (4) FSRA.

379 Section 170 FSRA.

380 The FSCA website list all the enforcement determinations handed down over a period of 13 years. https://www.fsca.co.za/Enforcement-Matters/Pages/default.aspx (last visited 13 June 2019).

381 Sections 175 to 177 FSRA.

The Tribunal was established for the purposes of reconsidering decisions made by a financial services regulator, Ombud Council and authorised financial services provider, as well as decisions in relation to a specific person by a market infrastructure. Members of the Tribunal must include at least 2 persons who are retired judges or are persons with suitable expertise and experience in law; and at least 2 other persons with experience or expert knowledge of financial products, financial services, financial instruments, market infrastructures or the financial system. The Tribunal may by order, set the decision before it aside and remit the matter to the decision-maker for further consideration. The Tribunal may also set aside the decision before it and substitute it with the decision of the Tribunal.

As in the case of supervision, the powers and duties of a regulatory authority (e.g. FSCA) in terms of the relevant financial sector law are to be taken as being in addition to the powers and duties it has in terms of the FSRA.

Conclusion

The genesis of public capital markets in South Africa was the capital formation needs of the mining industry. Over the years, the markets have evolved to serve most of the sectors of the economy.

As an initial step to this work the author has laid out and considered the policy context underpinning the regulatory approach. The focus then shifts to the continuing and emerging regulatory and supervisory framework. Although South Africa is currently ranked a lowly 46 in securities regulation in the world and there is some concern about the direction and consequences of aspects of the reform current underway, the point is made that all things considered, the ecosystem for regulation and supervision across the capital markets value chain has worked and continues to work reasonably well. Many aspects of regulatory framework which have been discussed were only recently introduced, hence there is a limited track record of implementation. The author's approach has therefore been to comment and analyse the new developments against best practice.

For their part policy makers have always stressed their intention to ensure that the regulatory framework has remains compatible with best practice. For this purpose they have regularly carried out periodic and targeted reviews, an example of the latter being the detailed studies triggered by the GFC.

Amendments and enhancements have been made to the relevant laws as some deficiencies were identified and also as a consequence of the observance of the precepts of best practice as communicated from time to time by, e.g.

IOSCO and peer comparison. Local competition, for instance, has proved to be an obdurate issue and remains unresolved. Although new players have been licensed, the policy makers have stopped short of implementing the full pro-competition measures recommended in MiFID.

Going forward, specific challenges faced by the regulator include the regulation and supervision of multiple exchanges and financial market infrastructures which have different and technologically driven business models. These challenges have implications for the regulator's resources and skills.

The introduction of FSRA and the decision to consolidate the separate sectoral financial laws, is a major task for the policy and drafting teams. It will therefore be some time before certainty is restored to the sector.

Notes on the Author

B.L. (Hons); LLB; Juris Doctor; Attorney-and-Counsellor-at-Law, State of Illinois, USA; Attorney of the Supreme Court of South Africa. Positions previously held include: Deputy Chief Executive Officer, Financial Services Board of South Africa; Member of the Board of the International Organisation of Securities Commissions (IOSCO) and Vice-Chair of the IOSCO Growth & Emerging Markets Committee; Member of Monitoring Board of the International Financial Reporting Standards Foundation; Vice-Chair, International Securities & Capital Markets Committee, American Bar Association, Section of International Law; Member Standing Advisory Committee on Company Law, Department of Trade & Industry, South Africa. Currently an independent consultant and educator in financial, securities and capital markets regulation, corporate governance and strategic finance.

Bibliography

1. Klaus Schwab: World Economic Forum Global Competitiveness Report. http://www3.weforum.org/docs/GCR2017-2018/05FullReport/TheGlobalCompetitivenessReport2017%E2%80%932018.pdf (last visited 13 June 2019).
2. Reviewing the Regulation of Financial Markets in South Africa, Policy document explaining the Financial Markets Bill, 2011. http://www.treasury.gov.za/public%20comments/FMB/FMB%20policy%20document.pdf. 9 (last visited 3 June 2019).
3. Trading Economics: South Africa Rating. https://tradingeconomics.com/south-africa/rating (last visited 13 June 2019).

4. Amira Daoui: The Biggest Economy in Africa? https://www.waystocap.com/blog/nigeria-vs-south-africa-which-is-africas-biggest-economy/ (last visited 13 June 2019).
5. Brand South Africa: SA Economy Overview. https://www.brandsouthafrica.com/investments-immigration/business/economy/south-africa-economy-overview (last visited 13 June 2019).
6. Shakill Hassan: South African Capital Markets: An overview. https://econrsa.org/system/files/publications/working_papers/working_paper_391.pdf (last visited 13 June 2019).
7. South African History Online: The Johannesburg Stock Exchange is Established. https://www.sahistory.org.za/dated-event/johannesburg-stock-exchange-established (last visited 13 June 2019).
8. JSE Market Highlights. https://www.jse.co.za/content/JSEEquityMarketWeeklyStatisticsItems/JSE%20Markets'%20Weekly%20Statistics%2020181026.xlsx (last visited 13 June 2019).
9. South African Reserve Bank: Current Market Rates. https://www.resbank.co.za/Research/Rates/Pages/CurrentMarketRates.aspx (last visited 13 June 2019).
10. Eamonn Ryan: Alt X Listings Boom Sustainable. https://www.entrepreneurmag.co.za/advice/personal-wealth/investing/alt-x-listings-boom-sustainable/ (last visited 13 June 2019).
11. Bank for international Settlements: Basel 3: A global regulatory framework for more resilient banks and banking systems. https://www.bis.org/publ/bcbs189.htm (last visited 13 June 2019).
12. KPMG: Basel 3: Issues and Implications. https://www.iia.nl/SiteFiles/basell-III-issues-implications.pdf (last visited 13 June 2019).
13. Justine Davies: Global Financial Crisis – What caused it and how the world responded. https://www.canstar.com.au/home-loans/global-financial-crisis 9 (last visited 13 June 2019).
14. IOSCO's Objectives and Principles for Securities Regulation: https://www.iosco.org/library/pubdocs/pdf/IOSCOPD323.pdf (last visited 13 June 2019).
15. IMF South Africa: Financial System Stability Assessment, Including Report on the Observance of Standards and Codes on the Following Topic: Securities Regulation. https://www.imf.org/external/pubs/ft/scr/2008/cr08349.pdf page 10 (last visited 13 June 2019).
16. Unidroit Convention On Substantive Rules For Intermediated Securities (Geneva, 2009) Last Updated: 27 September 2013. https://www.unidroit.org/instruments/international-sales/103-instruments/capital-markets/capital-markets-geneva-convention/178-unidroit-convention-on-substantive-rules-for-intermediated-securities-geneva-2009 (last visited 13 June 2019).

17. National Treasury: A Safer Financial Sector to Serve South Africa Better. http://www.treasury.gov.za/documents/national%20budget/2011/a%20safer%20financial%20sector%20to%20serve%20south%20africa%20better.pdf (last visited 13 June 2019).
18. Brooke Masters: Regulator's Light Touch Led to Failure. https://www.ft.com/content/2bf14c52-24ce-11e1-bfb3-00144feabdc0 (last visited 13 June 2019).
19. Andre Clark and Jill Treanor: I was wrong about the Economy. Sort of. (Greenspan) https://www.theguardian.com/business/2008/oct/24/economics-creditcrunch-federal-reserve-greenspan (last visited 13 June 2019).
20. The Economist: Northern Rock: Lessons of the Fall. https://www.economist.com/briefing/2007/10/18/lessons-of-the-fall (last visited 13 June 2019).
21. Reserve Bank of Australia: Global Financial Crisis. https://www.rba.gov.au/education/resources/explainers/the-global-financial-crisis.html (last visited 13 June 2019).
22. Martin Buffet: How do CDOs and CDSs influence the crisis of 2008. Lingnan Journal of Banking, Finance and Economics. http://commons.ln.edu.hk/cgi/viewcontent.cgi?article=1032&context=ljbfe (last visited 13 June 2019).
23. Stephen Brown: The Role of Hedge Funds in Financial Crises. http://w4.stern.nyu.edu/blogs/sternonfinance/2008/11/the-role-of-hedge-funds-in-fin.html (last visited 13 June 2019).
24. IMF: Making Over-the Counter Derivatives Safer. The Role of Central Counter-Parties. https://www.imf.org/~/media/Websites/IMF/imported-flagship-issues/external/pubs/ft/GFSR/2010/01/pdf/_chap3pdf.ashx (last visited 13 June 2019).
25. Johnny Hopkins: Derivatives Are Financial Weapons Of Mass Destruction. https://acquirersmultiple.com/2017/02/warren-buffett-derivatives-are-financial-weapons-of-mass-destruction/ (last visited 13 June 2019).
26. Essays, UK: Impact of the Global Economic crisis on the Automotive Industry. https://www.ukessays.com/essays/economics/impact-of-global-economic-crisis-on-automotive-industry-economics-essay.php (last visited 13 June 2019).
27. World Bank: The Impact of the Global Financial Crisis on Financial Markets in Sub-Saharan Africa. http://siteresources.worldbank.org/INTAFRSUMAFTPS/Resources/CrisisNote3.pdf, page 3 (last visited 13 June 2019).
28. Dr Hendrik Nel, South African Reserve Bank, Commentary: Financial Innovation and a New Economics of Banking: Lessons from the Financial Crisis. https://www.resbank.co.za/Lists/News%20and%20Publications/Attachments/51/Hendrik+Nel.pdf (last visited 13 June 2019).
29. IMF: Impact of the Global Financial Crisis on Sub-Saharan Africa https://www.imf.org/external/pubs/ft/books/2009/afrglobfin/ssaglobalfin.pdf (last visited 13 June 2019).

30. Marc Ashton: DealStream: as the FSB Saw IT. https://www.fin24.com/companies/dealstream-as-the-fsb-saw-it-20081008 (last visited 13 June 2019).
31. State v Arthur Brown. The Supreme Court of Appeal of South Africa, case number 681/2013.
32. Executive Officer: Financial Services Board vs Dynamic Wealth Limited and Others. 2012 (1) SA 453 (SCA).
33. Chantelle Benjamin: First Strut's Web of Deceit Unravels. https://mg.co.za/article/2013-08-02-00-first-struts-web-of-deceit-unravels (last visited 13 June 2019).
34. Bruce Cameron: First Strut investors stand to lose R 800 million. https://www.iol.co.za/personal-finance/my-money/banking/first-strut-investors-stand-to-lose-r800m-1567468 (last visited 13 June 2019).
35. JSE Listings Requirements. https://www.jse.co.za/content/JSERulesPoliciesandRegulationItems/JSE%20Debt%20Listings%20Requirements%20Service%20Issue%2025.pdf (last visited 13 June 2019).
36. Hilary Joffe, Sunday Times: JSE Proposals Seek to tighten Bond Market Listing Requirements. http://futuregrowth.co.za/newsroom/jse-proposals-seek-to-tighten-bond-market-listing-rules/ (last visited 13 June 2019).
37. South African History Online: The Union of South Africa 1910. https://www.sahistory.org.za/topic/union-south-africa-1910 (last visited 13 June 2019).
38. Amanda Barratt and Pamela Snyman, update by Salona Lutchman: Researching South African Law. http://www.nyulawglobal.org/globalex/South_Africa1.html.
39. The Companies Act 71 of 2008.
40. Jill Treanor: Farewell to the FSA – and the bleak legacy of the light-touch regulator. https://www.theguardian.com/business/2013/mar/24/farewell-fsa-bleak-legacy-light-touch-regulator (last visited 13 June 2019).
41. Mtende Mhango: Approach with Care when Considering Twin Peaks. https://www.iol.co.za/business-report/opinion/approach-with-care-when-considering-twin-peaks-1656994 (last visited 13 June 2019).
42. National Treasury: Implementing a Twin Peaks Model of Financial Regulation in South Africa, 1 February 2013, page 23. http://www.treasury.gov.za/twinpeaks/20131211%20-%20Item%203%20Roadmap.pdf (last visited 13 June 2019).
43. National Treasury: Twin Peaks in South Africa. https://old.juta.co.za/media/filestore/2015/03/2014_12_12_Response_document.pdf (last visited 13 June 2019).
44. Securities Regulation in a Nutshell, 10th edition, ISBN: 978-0-314-18798-7.
45. African Markets: About the Johannesburg Stock Exchange. https://www.african-markets.com/en/stock-markets/jse/about (last visited 13 June 2019).
46. Financial Sector Regulation Act 9 of 2017.
47. Financial Markets Act 19 of 2012.

48. FSCA: About the FSB. www.fsca.co.za (last visited 13 June 2019).
49. David Tricott and Adam M. Howard, Skadden, Arps, Slate, Meagher: Initial Public Offerings Law Review. https://www.skadden.com/-/media/files/publications/2017/06/united_kingdom_ipo.pdf (last visited 13 June 2019).
50. Treasury Comments on issues Raised during the Consultation Period for the Financial Markets Bill. http://www.treasury.gov.za/legislation/bills/2012/FMB/FMB%20Explanatory%20Memorandum.pdf (last visited 13 June 2019).
51. 2018 Financial Markets Review. http://www.treasury.gov.za/publications/other/2018_FMR_07.pdf (last visited 13 June 2019).
52. National Treasury: Secondary Market Making Obligation on The R2023 (7.75per cent:2023) by Primary Dealers In Fixed Rate Government Bonds of the Republic of South Africa. http://www.treasury.gov.za/comm_media/press/2012/2012090501.pdf (last visited 13 June 2019).
53. National Treasury: MEDIA STATEMENT Electronic Trading Platform for RSA Government Bonds. http://www.treasury.gov.za/comm_media/press/2014/2104091902%20-%20Media%20Statement%20ETP%20for%20RSA%20Government%20Bonds.pdf (last visited 13 June 2019).
54. SA Government Gazette: Financial Markets Act: Amendments: JSE Bond Electronic Trading Platform Rules. https://www.gov.za/sites/default/files/41773__bn91.pdf (last visited 13 June 2019).
55. Credit Rating Services Act 24 of 2012.
56. GN 141 of 25 February 2015: Declaration of Hedge Fund Business as a Collective Investment Scheme (Government Gazette No. 38503).
57. Reforming the Listed Property Sector in South Africa. http://www.treasury.gov.za/publicper cent20comments/REITSper cent20discussionper cent20document.pdf (last visited 13 June 2019).
58. Taxation Laws Amendment Act, 2012 (Act No. 22 of 2012). https://www.sars.gov.za/AllDocs/LegalDoclib/AmendActs/LAPD-LPrim-AA-2012-03%20-%20Taxation%20Laws%20Amendment%20Act%202012.pdf (last visited 13 June 2019).
59. Fin24: Why it makes sense to invest in REITS. https://www.fin24.com/Economy/why-it-makes-sense-to-invest-in-reits-20180328 (last visited 13 June 2019).
60. Financial Services Board Notice 42 of 2014, Collective Investment Schemes Control Act, 2002: Conditions for the Winding up of a Collective Investment Scheme in Property under Certain Circumstances.
61. Financial Services Board Notice 92 of 2014, Collective Investment Schemes Control Act, 2002.
62. ESMA publishes MiFID II Supervisor Briefing on Suitability. https://www.esma.europa.eu/press-news/esma-news/esma-publishes-mifid-ii-supervisory-briefing-suitability (last visited 13 June 2019).

63. Jonathan Fourie: "A New Playing Field with the Introduction of FSCA" http://www.fia.org.za/blog/a-new-playing-field-with-the-introduction-of-the-fsca/ (last visited 13 June 2019).
64. ASIC: How We Operate. https://asic.gov.au/about-asic/what-we-do/how-we-operate/ (last visited 13 June 2019).
65. Current SEC Commissioners. https://www.sec.gov/Article/about-commissioners.html (last visited 13 June 2019).
66 National Treasury: Commissioner and Deputy Commissioners of the Financial Sector Conduct Authority Pretoria. http://www.treasury.gov.za/careers/Commissioner%20and%20Deputy%20of%20the%20Financial%20Sector%20Conduct%20Authority.pdf (last visited 13 June 2019).
67. FSCA: Meet the Commissioners. https://www.fsca.co.za/Pages/Commissioners.aspx (last visited 13 June 2019).
68. Money Marketing: FSCA Commissioner appoints Divisional Executives. https://www.moneymarketing.co.za/fsca-commissioner-appoints-divisional-executives/.
69. Ra'eesa Pather: "Everything you need to know about the FIC Amendment Bill." Mail & Guardian. https://mg.co.za/article/2017-01-31-crib-notes-everything-you-need-to-know-about-the-fic-amendment-bill/ (last visited 13 June 2019).
70. The Regulatory Strategy of the FSCA for the period October 2018 to September 2021. https://www.fsca.co.za/Documents/FSCA_Strategy_2018.pdf (last visited 13 June 2019).
71. Financial Intelligence Centre Act 38 of 2001 as read with Financial Intelligence Centre Amendment Act 1 of 2017.
72. Myles Udland: Facebook has a New Class Structure and Mark Zuckerberg is Still in Control. https://www.businessinsider.com/facebook-new-stock-structure-2016-4?IR=T (last visited 13 June 2019).
73. Naspers: The Naspers Voting Control Structure Ensures Continued Independence of the Group. https://www.naspers.com/about/control-structure (last visited 13 June 2019).
74. Broad-Based Black Economic Empowerment Act 53 of 2003.
75. Business Day TV: The reason BEE trusts are under investigation. https://www.businesslive.co.za/bd/companies/2019-04-24-watch-the-reason-bee-trusts-are-under-investigation/ (last visited 13 June 2019).
76. Basel Committee on Banking Supervision: Global Systemically Important Banks: Assessment Methodology and the Additional Loss Absorbency Requirement. https://www.bis.org/publ/bcbs201.pdf (last visited 13 June 2019).
77. Reuters: JSE Tightens Rules on Single Stock Futures. https://www.reuters.com/article/jse-futures/jse-tightens-rules-on-single-stock-futures-report-idUSL362877720090203 (last visited 13 June 2019).

78. Exchange Traded Notes JSE. https://www.jse.co.za/trade/equity-market/exchange-traded-products/exchange-traded-notes (last visited 13 June 2019).
79. Unit Trusts Control Act 54 of 1981.
80. JSE: Exchange Traded Funds. https://www.jse.co.za/trade/equity-market/exchange-traded-products/exchange-traded-funds (last visited 13 June 2019).
81. Johny Lambiris: Why Active Management Beats Passive in South Africa. https://www.prudential.co.za/insights/articlesreleases/why-active-management-beats-passive-in-south-africa/ (last visited 13 June 2019).
82. Desmond Pace: Active Versus Passive Investing: An Empirical Study of the US and European Mutual Funds and ETF's. https://www.emeraldinsight.com/doi/abs/10.1108/S1569-375920160000097006 (last visited 13 June 2019).
83. SARB Inward Listings. https://www.resbank.co.za/RegulationAndSupervision/FinancialSurveillanceAndExchangeControl/FAQs/Pages/Inward%20listings.aspx (last visited 13 June 2019).
84. Santoshi hawla: What is the difference Between Closed End and Open Ended Funds https://www.quora.com/What-is-the-difference-between-closed-and-open-ended-funds (last visited 13 June 2019).
85. Model (CIS) Deed. https://www.fsca.co.za/Regulated%20Entities/Regulated%20Entities%20Documents/CISCA%20-%20Model%20Deed%20for%20CIS%20in%20Property.pdf (last visited 13 June 2019).
86. BN 90 of 8 August 2014 (Government Gazette No. 37895). (CISs in securities).
87. GN 572 of 16 May 2008. (Collective Investment Schemes in Property).
88. BN 65 of 20 June 2014 (Government Gazette No. 37740). (Participation bonds).
89. South Africa Financial Sector Assessment Program Detailed Assessment of Implementation on the IOSCO Objectives and Principles of Securities Regulation. https://www.imf.org/external/pubs/ft/scr/2015/cr1557.pdf (last visited 13 June 2019).
90. Association for Savings and Investment South Africa. https://www.asisa.org.za/ (last visited 13 June 2019).
91. Martin Hesse: How Collective Investment Schemes are Classified. https://www.iol.co.za/personal-finance/how-collective-investments-are-classified-10406565 (last visited 13 June 2019).
92. Methodology for Assessing Compliance with IOSCO Principles. https://www.iosco.org/library/pubdocs/pdf/IOSCOPD562.pdf, page 192 (last visited 13 June 2019).
93. Code of Conduct for Authorised Users, 2005, BN 20 In Government Gazette 27231 of 31 January 2005.
94. South African Institute of Stockbrokers. https://www.sais.co.za/ (last visited 13 June 2019).
95. Financial Advisory and Intermediary Services Act 37 of 2002.

96. BN 194 of 15 December 2017: Determination of Fit and Proper Requirements (Government Gazette 41321).
97. BN 79 of 8 August 2003: Codes of Conduct for Administrative and Discretionary FSPS.
98. Long Term Insurance Act, 1998 (Act 52 of 1998).
99. Short-Term Insurance Act (Act 53 of 1998).
100. Pension Funds Act 24 of 1956.
101. Friendly Societies Act 25 of 1956.
102. Gareth Stokes: It takes years to undo a financial scandal. https://www.fanews.co.za/article/life-insurance/9/general/1202/it-takes-years-to-undo-a-financial-scandal/104 (last visited 13 June 2019).
103. BN 106 of 2008 (Regulatory Examinations).
104. Stephanie McKenzie: Regulatory Examinations, an Overview. http://financialmarketsjournal.co.za/oldsite/13thedition/printedarticles/regulatoryexams.htm (last visited 13 June 2019).
105. National Treasury: Regulating Over-The-Counter Derivatives Markets in South Africa. http://www.treasury.gov.za/otc/Regulating%20over-the-counter%20(OTC)%20derivates%20markets%20in%20South%20Africa.pdf (last visited 13 June 2019).
106. Criteria for Authorisation of ODPs. https://www.fsca.co.za/Notices/Conduct%20Standard%201%20of%202018%20-%20%20Criteria%20for%20Authorisation%20of%20ODPs.pdf (last visited 13 June 2019).
107. FSB Reviews Financial Vulnerabilities and Deliverables for G20 Summit. http://www.fsb.org/2018/10/fsb-reviews-financial-vulnerabilities-and-deliverables-for-g20-summit/ (last visited 13 June 2019).
108. National Credit Act 34 of 2005.
109. IMF Shadow Banking and Market Based Finance Tobias Adrian, International Monetary Fund. Helsinki September 14, 2017. https://www.imf.org/en/News/Articles/2017/09/13/sp091417-shadow-banking-and-market-based-finance (last visited 13 June 2019).
110. Amit Mudgill: BSE creates history! Exchange lists at Rs 1,085, 34.62per cent premium over issue price. https://economictimes.indiatimes.com/markets/stocks/news/bse-creates-history-exchange-lists-at-rs-1085-34-62-premium-over-issue-price/articleshow/56947266.cms (last visited 13 June 2019).
111. Amit Lolwai: Which Is the Oldest Stock Exchange in the World. https://timesofindia.indiatimes.com/Which-is-the-oldest-stock-exchange-in-the-world/articleshow/1491593.cms? (last visited 13 June 2019).
112. WFE Members. https://www.world-exchanges.org/membership-events (last visited 13 June 2019).

113. African Markets. https://www.african-markets.com/en/stock-markets/bvmt/tunis-stock-exchange-a-new-member-of-the-world-federation-of-exchanges (last visited 13 June 2019).
114. Economy Watch: Stock Markets in Sub-Saharan Africa … http://www.economywatch.com/stock-markets-in-world/sub-saharan-africa.html (last visited 13 June 2019).
115. WFE Members and Affiliates. https://www.world-exchanges.org/membership-events (last visited 13 June 2019).
116. List of Stock Exchanges in Latin America and the Caribbean. https://stocknewser.blogspot.com/2012/03/list-of-stock-exchanges-in-latin.html (last visited 13 June 2019).
117. James Hamilton: Markets in Financial Instruments Directive (MiFID): Broad Reforms to EU Financial Services Regulation. http://business.cch.com/securitiesLaw/news/MiFID%20whitepaper.pdf (last visited 13 June 2019).
118. The G20 Seoul Summit Declaration, 11–12 November 2010. https://www.treasury.gov/resource-center/international/Documents/1%20%20FINAL%20SEOUL%20COMMUNIQUE.pdf (last visited 13 June 2019).
119. G20 Leaders Statement Pittsburgh Statement. http://www.g20.utoronto.ca/2009/2009communique0925.html.
120. IOSCO Task Force Requirements for Wholesale Market Conduct. https://www.iosco.org/library/pubdocs/pdf/IOSCOPD563.pdf (last visited 13 June 2019).
121. 2018 Financial Markets Review. https://www.fsca.co.za/Regulatory%20Frameworks/Temp/2018%20Financial%20Markets%20Review.pdf (last visited 13 June 2019).
122. Regulatory Issues Raised by the Impact of Technological Changes on Market Integrity and Efficiency Consultation Report. http://www.iosco.org/library/pubdocs/pdf/IOSCOPD354.pdf (last visited 13 June 2019).
123. SME Financing Through Capital Markets Final Report. http://www.iosco.org/library/pubdocs/pdf/IOSCOPD493.pdf (last visited 13 June 2019).
124. JSE Limited / The Registrar of Securities Services: ZAR X Exchange Licence – Case Number A8/2016.
125. JSE Limited and 4 Africa Exchange (Ptyo LTD and The Registrar of Securities Services and ZAR X (Pty) Limited – Case Number A25/2016.
126. 4 Africa Exchange (Pty) Limited and The Registrar of Securities Services, ZAR X (Pty) Limited, L.T.C. Harms N.O., Afrifocus Securities (Pty) Limited, Anchor Securities Stockbrokers (Pty) Limited, Saxo Capital Markets South Africa (Pty) limited, Senwes Limited and Senwesbel Limited: Case 17/20474 (High Court of South Africa, South Gauteng).

127. Phillip Stafford: What is MiFID II and How Will it Affect EU's financial industry? https://www.ft.com/content/ae935520-96ff-11e7-b83c-9588e51488a0 (last visited 13 June 2019).
128. Sarah Jane Mahmud, Alison Williams and Ben Elliott: The Future Of Investment Research Post-MiFID II. https://www.bloomberg.com/professional/blog/future-investment-research-post-mifid-ii/ (last visited 13 June 2019).
129. BN 68 of 11 July 2014: Financial Services Board: Directive and Guideline No. 1 of 2014: Directive and Guideline Regarding Infrastructures Provided by Companies Facilitating Trading in Their Own Securities.
130. Brett Landman: What is Satrix 40? https://www.fin24.com/money/money-clinic/what-is-satrix-40-20111110 (last visited 13 June 2019).
131. Financial Markets Act Regulations GNR 98 of 9 February 2018 (Government Gazette 41433).
132. BN 92 of 8 August 2014: Advertising, Marketing and Information Disclosure Requirements for Collective Investment Schemes (Government Gazette 37895 – CIS Information Disclosure Requirements).
133. Companies Regulations, 2011 GN R 351 of 26 April 2011 (Government Gazette 34239) as amended by GN R 619 of 20 August 2013 (Government Gazette 36759) and GN R 82 of 5 February 2014 (Government Gazette 37299).
134. Genevieve Wood: What is Chi-X and How Does it work? http://blog.openmarkets.com.au/what-is-chi-x-and-how-does-it-work (last visited 13 June 2019).
135. Roy Cokayne: Action Groups Mobilise to Recoup R4.5 billion. https://www.iol.co.za/business-report/companies/action-groups-mobilise-to-recoup-r45-billion-13902758 (last visited 13 June 2019).
136. Martin Hesse: Ombud Orders Advisers to Pay Back the Money. https://www.iol.co.za/personal-finance/ombud-orders-advisers-to-pay-back-the-money-13601546 (last visited 13 June 2019).
137. G20 Leaders Pittsburgh Statement. http://www.g20.utoronto.ca/2009/2009communique0925.html (last visited 13 June 2019).
138. IOSCO Task Force Requirements for Wholesale Market Conduct. https://www.fsca.co.za/Regulatory%20Frameworks/Temp/2018%20Financial%20Markets%20Review.pdf (last visited 13 June 2019).
139. 2018 Financial Markets Review. https://www.fsca.co.za/Regulatory%20Frameworks/Temp/2018%20Financial%20Markets%20Review.pdf (last visited 13 June 2019).
140. Natalie Sherman: Elliott Management: The hedge fund not afraid of a fight. https://www.bbc.com/news/business-39630871 (last visited 13 June 2019).
141. SEC Gov: Cumulative Voting. https://www.sec.gov/fast-answers/answers-cumulativevotehtm.html (last visited 13 June 2019).

142. G20/OECD Code on Corporate Governance. http://www.oecd.org/corporate/principles-corporate-governance.htm (last visited 13 June 2019).
143. First King Report on Corporate Governance (published 29 November 1994). https://www.iodsa.co.za/page/kingIII (last visited 13 June 2019).
144. King Code on Corporate Governance for South Africa. https://c.ymcdn.com/sites/www.iodsa.co.za/resource/resmgr/king_iv/King_IV_Report/IoDSA_King_IV_Report_-_WebVe.pdf (last visited 13 June 2019).
145. Auditing Professions Act 26 of 2005.
146. Joanne Matison: Director and Auditor Rotation in South Africa. http://www.mondaq.com/southafrica/x/590796/Audit/Director+and+auditor+rotation+in+South+Africa (last visited 13 June 2019).
147. Live Mint: Satyam case: Sebi bans PwC entities from auditing listed firms for two years. https://www.livemint.com/Companies/KlbBm6VhxhQQswdgT9bycK/Satyam-case-Sebi-bans-PwC-entities-from-auditing-listed-fir.html (last visited 13 June 2019).
148. CPSS Red Book: Payment, Clearing and Settlement Systems in South Africa. https://www.bis.org/cpmi/publ/d105_za.pdf (last visited 13 June 2019).
149. The Joint Forum CORE PRINCIPLES CROSS-SECTORAL COMPARISON Nov 2001. https://www.bis.org/publ/joint03.pdf (last visited 13 June 2019).
150. IOSCO Online Self-Assessment Questionnaire. https://www.iosco.org/online-methodology-2017/ (last visited 13 June 2019).
151. Guidelines to Emerging Market Regulators Regarding Requirements for Minimum Entry and Continuous Risk-Based Supervision of Market Intermediaries Final Report. Page 10, http://www.iosco.org/library/pubdocs/pdf/IOSCOPD314.pdf (last visited 13 June 2019).
152. Harmony Gold Mining Company Fined. https://www.fsca.co.za/Enforcement-Matters/Documents/EC_Signed%20Judgment_Harmony%20Gold%20Mining%20Company%20Limited_2018-10-04.pdf (last visited 13 June 2019).
153. State vs Jeffrey Israel Levenstein, Appeal Court case 809/12. http://www.justice.gov.za/sca/judgments/sca_2013/sca2013-147.pdf (last visited 13 June 2019).
154. Multilateral Memorandum of Understanding concerning Consultation and Cooperation and the Exchange of information adopted May 2002 and revised May 2012. https://www.iosco.org/library/pubdocs/pdf/IOSCOPD386.pdf (last visited 13 June 2019).
155. Enhanced Multilateral Memorandum of Understanding (EMMoU) adopted in 2016, in the years to come. https://www.iosco.org/about/pdf/Text-of-the-EMMoU.pdf (last visited 13 June 2019).
156. FSCA Enforcement Determinations. https://www.fsca.co.za/Enforcement-Matters/Pages/default.aspx (last visited 13 June 2019).

www.ingramcontent.com/pod-product-compliance
Ingram Content Group UK Ltd.
Pitfield, Milton Keynes, MK11 3LW, UK
UKHW040729170926
15229UKWH00005B/12

9 789004 395886